How to Become a Scottish Police Officer

www.How2Become.com

As part of this product you have also received FREE access to online tests that will help you to pass the Scottish Police Officer Tests.

To gain access, simply go to:

www.MyPsychometricTests.co.uk

Get more products for passing any test at:

www.How2Become.com

Orders: Please contact How2Become Ltd, Suite 14, 50 Churchill Square Business Centre, Kings Hill, Kent ME19 4YU.

You can order through Amazon.co.uk under ISBN: 9781912370337, via the website www.How2Become.com or through Gardners.com.

ISBN: 9781912370337

First published in 2018 by How2Become Ltd.

Typeset for How2Become Ltd by Gemma Butler.

Disclaimer

Every effort has been made to ensure that the information contained within this guide is accurate at the time of publication. How2Become Ltd is not responsible for anyone failing any part of any selection process as a result of the information contained within this guide. How2Become Ltd and their authors cannot accept any responsibility for any errors or omissions within this guide, however caused. No responsibility for loss or damage occasioned by any person acting, or refraining from action, as a result of the material in this publication can be accepted by How2Become Ltd.

The information within this guide does not represent the views of any third party service or organisation.

Contents

Introduction

Hello, and welcome to *How to Become a Scottish Police Officer*. In this guide, we'll give you a comprehensive overview on how you can join Police Scotland. From application form all the way to your final interview, we'll break down the entire process. By the end of this book, you will have absolutely no doubts over how you can gain a position within Police Scotland.

The selection process to join the police is highly competitive. Of the enormous numbers that apply, only a few will be successful. You could view this as a worrying statistic, or alternatively you could view it that you are determined to be one of the few who are successful. Armed with this insider's guide, you have certainly taken the first step to passing the police officer selection process.

To make things easier for you, our guide has been split up into useful sections. The benefit of this is that it will allow you to prepare for each stage individually. Read each section carefully and take notes as you progress. Don't ever give up on your dreams; if you really want to join Police Scotland, then you can do it. The way to approach the police officer selection process is to embark on a programme of in-depth preparation, and this guide will show you exactly how to do that.

The Scottish police officer selection process is not easy to pass, unless of course, you spend a decent amount of time preparing. Your preparation must be focused in the right areas, and also be comprehensive enough to give you every chance of success. You must also develop your own skills and experiences around the Police Scotland core competencies. Many candidates who apply to join the police will be unaware that the core competencies even exist. As you progress through this guide you will find that these important elements of the police officer role form the foundations of your preparation. In chapter 3 of this book, we will give you a full breakdown of all the Police Scotland core competencies, and why they are so important.

If you need any further help with passing the Police Scotland selection process, then we also offer a wide range of products which can assist you. These include guides on how to pass the language, numerical and information handling tests, plus an interview guide. These are all available via our website, www. How2Become.com.

Once again, thank you for your custom and we wish you every success in your pursuit to becoming a police officer.

Work hard, stay focused and, secure your dream career...

Best wishes,

The how2become team

The How2Become Team

Police Scotland: A Brief History

Before we begin breaking down the selection process, it's important to shed some light on what Police Scotland actually is, and how it came into being. When applying for any job, employers will expect you to have researched the company beforehand, and therefore it should come as no surprise that Police Scotland does the same. During the selection process, whether it's part of the application stage or the interview, you'll need to demonstrate your research and knowledge. So, with this in mind, here's a bit of information on how Police Scotland operates:

Police Scotland was established on the 1st April 2013. Previously to this, Scottish policing operated under a system of eight regional forces, which were replaced by one unified force in Police Scotland. Police Scotland is the second largest force in the entire UK, with the Metropolitan Police being the largest.

In terms of hierarchy, Police Scotland is led by a Chief Constable. Below the Chief Constable are Deputy Chief Constables, Assistant Chief Constables and Directors, and below this are police officers, special constables and response officers. Regardless of rank, the purpose and intention of every person working within Police Scotland is to safeguard the people of Scotland, and protect their community. The Police Scotland HQ is based in Fife, where you can also find the Scottish Police College. All training for Scottish police officers will be done on the premises of the Scottish Police College. So, if you are successful in applying, then you can expect to spend a significant period of time here.

Police Scotland's Forward Command Base is at Randolphfield in Stirling. This command base ensures the Police Scotland command team is able to oversee policing operations across the country. The Senior Leadership Team work from both sites.

Police Scotland took over responsibility for policing in Scotland from the eight former police forces, the Scottish Crime and Drug Enforcement Agency and the Association of Chief Police Officers in Scotland.

Police Scotland is structured into 13 locally-based divisions. Each division is led by a Local Police Commander. This person is tasked with ensuring that the policing specific to that area is up to scratch. Along with working as a regular police officer, there are also many specialist roles available within Police Scotland. This includes options to work in Major Crime investigation, Counter Terrorism, Intelligence and Public Protection, as well as many others. Alongside this, Police Scotland also offers operational support roles – such as Marine Policing and Air Support, amongst others.

Every year, Police Scotland publishes what is known as an Annual Police Plan, to ensure that they are delivering the best possible level of service to the Scottish Public. In this plan, the service outlines their yearly aims, strategies and priorities, for safeguarding the Scottish public.

Core Competencies

When attending any interview, one of the fundamental things that you need to consider is the core competencies of the organisation that you are applying to. This is extremely important in the police service, who have a very strict set of values, ethics, and behaviour for their employees. The police play an extremely important role in society, and need to ensure that they can behave with professionalism, decency, and integrity – so that the general public can trust in them. In order to guarantee this, Police Scotland have a specific code of conduct that they expect candidates to abide by. This code encompasses the core competencies, which are listed below:

Effective Communication
Communication is incredibly important when working in the police, and therefore it is essential that candidates can demonstrate an ability to put across their ideas in a clear and concise manner, in both written form and verbal. Working in the police will put you in contact with a wide variety of people from different backgrounds, and therefore it's vital that you can communicate effectively. Not only will you utilise your communication skills when dealing with members of the public, but you will also need to communicate with different members of the law enforcement team, and professionals from outside of the police – such as social workers or lawyers. You may also be asked to appear in court, where you will need to communicate verbally. Alternatively, your written reports could be used in court as evidence. These are just some of the many reasons that communication is essential for police officers.

A police officer who has **good communication** can:

- Communicate effectively in writing as well as verbally;

- Identify when it is appropriate to use certain styles of communication and language;

- Adapt their communication according to the individual(s) being addressed;

- Use grammar, spelling, and punctuation effectively and correctly;

- Listen carefully when they are being spoken to, taking note of essential information;

- Influence the behaviour of others in a positive way, using good communication.

Personal Effectiveness

Personal effectiveness roughly translates to taking responsibility and ensuring that you can achieve results to the level that Police Scotland expect. It's about making sure that your own standards are up to scratch, and that you are always looking to improve and better yourself. In order to do this, you must be able to demonstrate qualities such as commitment, perseverance, and integrity, as well as a strong drive to increase the quality of your performance. Naturally, this is very important when working in the police, who demand the highest possible standards of their employees. Every single member of the police service has a responsibility to maintain an impeccable standard of work, and be willing to adapt and grow with the changing demands of the police.

A police officer who has good **personal effectiveness** can:

- Take personal responsibility for achieving results to the highest possible standard;

- Show commitment, motivation and perseverance towards police tasks;

- Understand the need for change and be willing to adapt to new methods of police practice;

- Work within an agreed timeframe, setting realistic personal objectives and goals;

- Demonstrate integrity and professionalism, in line with the police code of ethics.

Team Working

Teamwork is extremely important when working in the police. Your ability to work in synchronisation with your colleagues, to create an effective and organised policing unit, will be paramount to the success of Police Scotland. The better police staff can work together, the stronger the level of care that you can provide to the public. Policing is not a one-person job. It takes the combined efforts of the entirety of Police Scotland to fight crime successfully. As an officer, you will need to call on the help of many other specialists working within the police, and in outside agencies, so it's essential that your team working skills are top notch.

A police officer who has good **team working skills** can:

- Develop good professional and personal relationships with colleagues;

- Participate in group activities and team-based exercises, playing an important role in these endeavours;

- Take the views and opinions of others into account, and is prepared to discuss the views of others in a polite and amicable fashion;

- Utilise an open, honest and supportive approach when assisting other colleagues;

- Accept that not all tasks need to be completed solo, and ask for help when appropriate.

Respect for Diversity

As a police officer, it's hugely important that you have respect for diversity. You certainly cannot work within the police service without this. This essentially involves considering and showing respect for the opinions, circumstances, and feelings of colleagues and members of the public, no matter their race, religion, position, background, circumstances, status, or appearance. It is essential that you can take an unbiased and fair-minded approach to dealing with every single member of the public, and that you can understand and respect the needs of people from different backgrounds. Remember that the police are there to serve every single law-abiding citizen, and not just people from select backgrounds, and therefore it's vital that you have a good understanding of every person's needs and beliefs.

A police officer with **respect for diversity** can:

- Respect the values and feelings of people from a diverse range of backgrounds;

- Treat every single person that they meet with the utmost respect and fairness;

- Be diplomatic when dealing with all members of the public;

- Understand the need to be sensitive to differing social, cultural and racial requirements;

- Immediately challenge any inappropriate or discriminatory behaviour.

Job Knowledge

Naturally, job knowledge is another essential competency. As in any line of work, it's extremely important for police employees to have a full and capable understanding of their role, what it involves, and what their key responsibilities and duties are. Obviously, this is something that will become much more apparent when you start working for the police, but you are still expected to have a basic knowledge when applying. Prior to application, you'll need to research into topics such as your local force's priorities, what training they offer, and the type of work that they do. You should expect to be asked questions based around these subjects during the interview.

A police officer with good **job knowledge** can:

- Show the assessors that they are aware of the physical and mental demands of working in the police;

- Demonstrate that they are aware of the behavioural standards of the police, and can act accordingly;

- Understand the importance of adhering to established police procedures and policies;

- Display an appreciation for all of the elements that go into working as a successful police officer, and make a sustained effort to go above and beyond expectations, whenever possible.

Personal Awareness
Personal awareness is a really important quality for a police officer to have. As officers of the law, it is vital that police employees can understand how their own behaviour has an impact on others. You need to act with empathy and diplomacy when dealing with members of the public, and with your own colleagues. The only way that you can do this is if you have a firm understanding of your own emotions. You must be able to recognise how your emotions can impact upon your performance, and how this could affect the way you deal with others. Working as a police officer is mentally taxing, as well as physically. There will be times when you aren't

in the best state of mind or mood, but it is vital that you can adopt ways of dealing with this, or of recognising when you need to take yourself away from a particular situation.

A police officer with good **personal awareness** can:

* Demonstrate a good understanding of how their behaviour impacts those around them;

* Deal with sensitive situations, in an appropriate and diplomatic manner;

* Listen to the views of others, and recognise flaws in their own methods or ideas;

* Learn how to manage their own emotions, and limit disruptive thoughts or feelings, so that their performance is consistent;

* Have confidence in their own ability to perform to a high standard.

Problem Solving

Problem solving is another essential competency. Much of police work involves using common sense to make decisions and draw logical conclusions. You must be someone who can think analytically and assess situations in a calm and logical fashion. Your judgement as a police officer is extremely important, and it's imperative that you can make logical use of evidence when it presents itself.

A police officer with good **problem solving** can:

* Gather information from a wide variety of sources, to help identify potential solutions to problems;

* Work within established police procedures and systems, to find solutions to problems;

- Assess the benefits and negatives of potential decisions;

- Justify their decisions with sound reasoning and logic;

- Accept responsibility for their decisions and learn from their own mistakes.

Service Delivery

Service delivery is all about focusing on the needs of the customer – which in this case is the general public. In a nutshell, service delivery means providing the public with the best possible care and service. Essentially, you need to be able to do your job to the highest standards and remember that safeguarding the public is your number one priority. In doing this, you will need to deal with complaints, learn how to reassure distressed individuals, and develop good relationships with community members of the area in which you are policing.

A police officer with good **service delivery** can:

- Evaluate the individual needs of specific customers;

- Prioritise requests from members of the public, taking into account ongoing tasks and projects;

- Develop a good relationship with members of the community;

- Respond to customer feedback in an appropriate manner;

- Ensure that members of the public feel valued and safeguarded by the police service.

Leadership

Leadership is an important quality for any police officer to have. As a police officer, it's essential that you can act as a role model for others, and lead by example. With this in mind, police officers need to behave in an exemplary fashion. This applies both at the station, and whilst out in public. In the latter example, it's very important that the public can look to officers for reassurance and guidance on the correct way to behave. You must act in a thoughtful and fair manner and be able to think through the implications of your decisions.

A police officer with good **leadership** can:

* Act as a role model and set a good example for others;

* Behave with integrity and professionalism, ensuring that all of their decisions are made with fairness in mind;

* Make big judgement calls when necessary and be prepared to take ownership for these decisions;

* Gain the trust of police colleagues, and members of the public.

Partnership Working
Partnership working is extremely important for the police service, and closely relates with teamwork. It's essential that the police service can work in tandem with partner agencies, to provide the best possible service to the public. Working in the police is all about taking a joint approach to solving problems. Whether that's with your own colleagues or with external staff, a problem shared is a problem halved. With this in mind, it's important that you are able to demonstrate a polite, open-minded and courteous approach to members of other agencies.

A police officer with good **partnership-working** skills can:

* Establish good relationships with staff from partner agencies;

* Respect and adhere to the organisational policies and expectations of partner agencies, when working with them;

* Utilise good teamworking skills to work in conjunction with staff from other agencies;

- Act as an exemplary representative of the police service, when working with partner agencies;

- Consider the views and opinions of others, when making decisions.

Why Are the Competencies So Important?

At this point, you might be thinking that these competencies aren't important for you yet, given that you are only applying for the job. Well, think again, because they are extremely important! The core competencies are an essential part of the job application process, and your chances of success very much rest on how well you understand them, and how well you can demonstrate them. Throughout the application process, the police service will be constantly testing you, looking for you to demonstrate the core competencies. The interview questions will be heavily focused around the competencies, and each one will require you to demonstrate a different competency. So, you need to revise each one extremely carefully. Not only that, but you need to try and think of past examples/times when you have demonstrated this competency, and used it to resolve an issue.

Along with this, you may also be asked some ethics-based questions, and questions based on the Police Scotland Standards of Professional Behaviour. These questions focus around the expectations of police officers, and your motivations for applying to the police. We highly recommend that you study the Police Scotland Standards of Professional Behaviour, and the code of ethics. We have listed both of these below:

Police Scotland Standards of Professional Behaviour

- **Authority, respect and courtesy**

It's integral for police officers to act with self-control and tolerance, and they must be able to treat every person that they meet with kindness and courtesy.

- **Equality and diversity**

Police officers must respect fairness and impartiality. They should never discriminate, and must only use force when necessary and proportionate.

- **Duties and responsibilities**

In order for police officers to perform to the best of their ability, they must perform diligently in every single task that they are given.

- **Honesty and integrity**

Police officers must act with honesty and integrity at all times, and must never abuse their position, or place themselves in a situation where their reputation might be compromised.

- **Orders and instructions**

Police officers must recognise that they are duty bound to only give and adhere to lawful orders and instructions, and must not participate in any behaviour which could be deemed otherwise.

- **Confidentiality**

In order for police officers to gain the trust and respect of the general public, they must treat information with respect, and only disclose said information in a correct and lawful manner, when appropriate.

- **Fitness for duty**

It's extremely important that officers can monitor their own performance, to ensure that they are up to the task of carrying out their responsibilities.

• **Discreditable conduct**

Police officers must never behave in a way which damages or discredits the reputation of Police Scotland, or undermines public confidence in the police.

• **Challenging and reporting improper conduct**

It's essential that police officers are able to take action and challenge any conduct which falls below the standards of professional behaviour for police officers.

Police Scotland Code of Ethics

• **Respect**

Respect is a core part of working for the police. It means taking pride in your team, and showing respect for every single person, regardless of their background, gender or culture. Police officers must be able to understand the importance of upholding the law and contributing to the professional reputation of Police Scotland.

Regardless of whom you are dealing with, whether it is an innocent person or a detained individual, you must treat them in a dignified, polite and respectful manner.

• **Fairness**

Police officers must be able to face every challenge that they meet whilst working for Police Scotland, with courage, tolerance and composure. It's essential that all employees of Police Scotland are able to promote positivity and unity within the community.

In the interests of fairness, police officers must be able to take an open-minded approach to all community and social issues, and carry out every single one of their duties in an impartial and non-discriminatory manner.

- **Human rights**

Understanding human rights is really important for police officers. It's integral to ensure that your actions as an officer are done in a way which shows respect for human rights, and does not breach this protocol.

All employees of Police Scotland must understand the appropriate use of force, and not utilise this in circumstances where it would not be deemed inappropriate, or illegitimate. Prior to making any decision which requires force, officers must be able to clearly think through their actions and whether they are necessary.

Furthermore, it's essential that officers understand that people have an equal right to liberty and security, and therefore do not encourage or allow any form of torture or degradation to any other person, whether that be a member of the public or a detainee.

Finally, it's essential that police officers understand the principle of 'innocent until proven guilty'.

- **Integrity**

Police officers must be able to recognise that their role, as an employee of Police Scotland, requires them to act with integrity at all times. It's imperative that police officers can behave in a manner that is reflective of the values of Police Scotland, and that they can take responsibility for their own behaviour.

In order to act as a role model, it's imperative that Police Scotland employees can put community service above their own personal goals, and do not participate in any behaviour that could be seen as compromising their impartiality – for example accepting gifts from members of the public, or favouring certain groups over others.

All employees of Police Scotland are expected to challenge any behaviour that they believe falls below the standards of the organisation.

Now that we've finished looking at what is expected of candidates for Police Scotland, let's get started with the application process. The very first step in the selection process is the application form.

Application Form

In order to apply for a job with Police Scotland, you will need to download an application form via their website. There are four forms in total which need to be completed, and these are as follows:

- An application form;

- A vetting form;

- An equality and diversity form;

- A posting preference questionnaire.

When submitting your application, you'll need to send off all four of the forms together. You should also remember that jobs with Police Scotland are in enormous demand. This means that the service receives an astronomical amount of applications, and as a result there is somewhat limited division space. You should always enquire with Police Scotland beforehand, to check that the division you want to work in has the capacity to take on new employees.

Why do you need to fill in an application form?
As with anything, understanding why you are completing a task is a good way to ensure that you can complete it to the best of your ability. There are lots of reasons for why Police Scotland require you to fill in an application form, but the primary reason is that the application form acts as an important sifting process. As mentioned, Police Scotland receives an enormous number of applications. They can't send every person who applies through to the initial interview, so the best way to narrow down the field is to weed out the unsuitable candidates as early as possible. The application form should give them a very good idea of whether you are the right type of person for the role.

When filling out the application form, you will need to make sure that you can meet the eligibility criteria. Naturally, the police have a very strict set of requirements that candidates must adhere to. Here's the eligibility criteria for Police Scotland.

Police Scotland: Eligibility Criteria

Age: You must be at least 17 years and 6 months old to apply, however candidates cannot be appointed as a police constable until they reach the age of 18. Police Scotland do not have an upper age limit when it comes to recruitment, but you should bear in mind that the majority of constables retire at around the age of 60.

Fitness: It's extremely important that candidates can demonstrate their physical fitness. In order to do this, Police Scotland will ask you to take a Multi-Stage fitness assessment, known as the MSFT. In order to pass this test, you will need to reach a level of 5.4.

Nationality and Residency: In order to apply for the role, you must be a British citizen, a citizen of the EEA or Switzerland, or have the right to live and work within the United Kingdom. Police Scotland also accept applications from commonwealth citizens and foreign nationals, but these individuals must be able to demonstrate that there no restrictions on their stay in the UK. Furthermore, you must be able to provide evidence of 3 years residency in the UK

Tattoos: While Police Scotland do allow tattoos, certain tattoos could present an obstacle to your appointment. If you have a tattoo which is deemed to be offensive or risks the reputation of the police service, then Police Scotland may refuse your application. Here are the rules surrounding tattoos:

• You cannot have tattoos on your face;

• If you do have a tattoo, then you will need to describe the nature, size and location of the tattoo to the police;

- Tattoos should not undermine the dignity of the officer;

- Tattoos should not risk causing offence to members of the public or anyone else, or invite provocation from others;

- Candidates will be rejected if they have tattoos which are considered to be rude, racist, lewd, homophobic, violent or intimidating.

Now that we've covered the eligibility criteria, let's look at the application form itself. Below we have provided you with a detailed breakdown on how the form should look, and how to go about impressing the assessors.

Police Scotland: Application Form

Section 1: Area of Residency

In the very first section of the application form, you'll be asked to select your current geographical area. This section should look similar to the below:

RESIDENCY			
To assist us in processing your application please select the area in which you currently reside.			
Aberdeen City, Aberdeenshire and Moray		Lotians and Scottish Borders	
Edinburgh		Ayrshire	
Highland and Islands		Lanarkshire	
Tayside		Argyll and West Dunbartonshire	
Forth Valley		Renfrewshire and Inverclyde	
Fife		Dumfries and Galloway	
Greater Glasgow		Out with Scotland	

Section 2: Personal Details

In the next section of the form, you'll need to fill in your personal details. This section should look similar to the below:

PERSONAL DETAILS	
First Name/s	
Surname/s	
Previous Name/s	
National Insurance Number	
Address	
Postcode	
Email address	

Contact Numbers	
Home	
Mobile	
Work	

Do you have a driving licence?	Yes / No
Licence Number	
Type of Licence	Full / Provisional Manual / Automatic
Expiry Date	

Section 3: Motivations and Values

The third section of the Police Scotland application form is arguably the most important part. In this section, you'll need to answer a series of questions regarding your reasons for wanting to join the police, and your understanding of Police Scotland as an organisation. Motivations and values questions are essentially questions which are formed around getting to know you as a person, to work out whether you are the right fit for the organisation. It's very important for the police to establish that you are applying for the right reasons. They don't want candidates who are applying 'to ride around in a police car with flashing lights'. They want candidates who are applying because they share the same values as the police – candidates who want to make a genuine difference in the community and protect the general public. So, you can expect questions such as:

'Tell me about why you are applying for this role.'

'What do you know about Police Scotland?'

'How do you think you can cope with the demands of the job?'

The motivations and values questions are likely to test you heavily on how well you've researched the job position. The police need to know that you understand what you are getting into, and won't quit as soon as the going gets tough. They also want to see that you have a genuine interest in their organisation. Conducting substantial research before application will show the police that you are serious about the role, and enthusiastic about the prospect of working for them.

Although you will be asked these types of questions during the application form, don't be surprised if you get one or two motivations and values questions during your actual interviews too. These types of questions are commonplace in any form of interview, as it's very important for employers to establish what kind of a person they would be hiring.

When answering these questions, you'll generally be given a limit of between 100-200 words with which to answer. This is not a lot of words, so you need to make every word count! Furthermore, it's **essential** that your grammar, spelling and punctuation are up to scratch. If the assessors take a look at your form and spot paragraphs riddled with errors, then your application will be discarded pretty much immediately. You need to check each answer thoroughly before submission.

There will be 7 questions in total during this section. Since you only have 200 words maximum per question, it's very important that you can keep your answers clear and concise. Take your time when answering, and think about the words that you are writing. Make sure that you avoid using any slang or colloquial jargon. Along with this, you also need to ensure that you answer **every single question**. If you leave any questions blank, then your application is likely to be rejected.

On the next pages we've included 5 sample questions from this part of the test. Remember that there will be 7 questions in total during the real thing! Try and answer each one yourself, using the textbox provided, and then compare it with our sample response below.

Q1. In 200 words or less, tell us about why you want to become a police officer.

Usually this is the first question that you can expect to encounter on your application form. The best response here, is to be honest! Think about the reasons for why you want to become a police officer. What has motivated you to apply? What is it about the police service that inspires you? Take a look at the goals and aims of Police Scotland on their website. Do you share these goals?

Sample Response

"I have wanted to become a police officer for almost four years now, and I can distinctly remember the time I decided this would be the job for me. I was walking through my local high street on my way to the gym on an early Saturday morning, when I noticed two police officers dealing with an aggressive and verbally abusive young man who, from what I understood later on, had been caught shoplifting from the newsagents in the high street. Whilst walking past, I stopped a few yards on, to see how the police officers would handle the situation.

The two police officers remained totally calm and in control of the situation, despite the abuse being directed at them by the man. Their body language was non-confrontational, and they appeared to be using well-thought out techniques to get him to calm down. From that point on I wanted to learn more about the role of a police officer. In addition to this, I have lived in the local community for virtually all my life, and I would feel proud to be part of an organisation that safeguards this community."

Q2. In 200 words or less, tell us about yourself and what qualities you believe you have, that will be relevant to the role of a police officer.

This is another very common question. Remember, the purpose of this form is to help Police Scotland find out more about who you are, and why you would be a great police officer. So, it's not unusual for them to just ask you this outright! Once again, your best response is to be honest in this situation. Think about what makes you a good fit for the role. What are your best qualities? How would they be of use to Police Scotland?

A word of caution when answering this, read the question! It's pretty easy here to go off on a tangent and reel off a big list of qualities that actually have nothing to do with the police service. Remember, you need to keep it relevant, and link your qualities back to what the police are looking for.

Sample Response

"To begin with, I am a hard-working, committed and highly-motivated person who prides himself on the ability to continually learn and develop new skills. I am 31 years old, and I currently work as a customer services manager for a transportation company. In addition to being a family person, I also have my own hobbies and interests, which include team sports such as football and also playing the guitar in a local band.

I am a loyal person, who has a strong track record at work for being reliable, flexible and customer-focused. My annual appraisals are consistently to a high standard and I am always willing to learn new skills. Before applying for this job, I studied the role of a police officer and also the role of the police service in depth, to make sure I was able to meet the requirements of the role. Having been working for my current employer for almost ten years now, I wanted to make sure that I had the potential to become a competent police officer before applying. Job stability is important to me and my family. If successful, I plan to stay in the police force for many years."

Q3. In 200 words or less, tell us what work you have done during your preparation for applying to become a police officer.

As we mentioned during the introduction, the police will want to know that you've conducted thorough preparation before applying. They want to see a level of dedication and enthusiasm right from the outset, and not just when you've got the job. Don't be surprised to encounter a question such as this, which directly challenges the amount of work you've put in beforehand. Remember too that there is enormous competition for jobs with Police Scotland. All of the other candidates (or the good ones anyway) will have put in strong amounts of preparation work beforehand – so you need to do your utmost to top this.

Sample Response

"I have carried out a huge amount of work, research and personal development prior to applying for this role. To begin with, I studied the role of a police officer, especially with regards to the core competencies. I wanted to make sure that I could meet the requirements of the role, so I asked myself whether I had sufficient evidence and experience to match each and every one of the core competencies.

Once I was certain that I had the experience in life, I started to find out more about the work the police carry out, both on a local and national level. I have studied your website in detail, and learnt as much as I possibly could about how you tackle crime, deal with the effects of it and also how you use statistics to drive down increasing crime trends in specific areas. In addition to reading and researching, I went along to my local police station to try and find out a bit more about the job, and the expectations that the public have from the police."

Q4. In 200 words or less, tell us about what your biggest strength is, and how this will benefit the police should we employ you.

This is a very common question, and it's also one that is highly likely to appear during the interview section. When answering this question, be careful. The interviewer will want you to focus on one major strength. They don't want an entire speech on how great you are and all of your qualities. Remember that you've only got 200 words. Focus on one major quality, and then elaborate on how you believe this can help the police.

Sample Response

"I believe that my biggest strength is in my ability to take leadership of difficult situations, and make crucial decisions. In my previous career, I have almost always worked in management positions, where I was required to make important decisions on a regular basis. I am well suited to dealing with large amounts of pressure and feel comfortable in making big decisions, as well as taking ownership and responsibility for these judgements.

I believe that this quality will strongly benefit me in my career as a police officer. I understand that working for the police involves large amounts of high-pressure decision making, and that officers must be able to remain calm and collected when the going gets tough. I feel that my decision-making skills would transfer over extremely well to the police, and that I would be able to benefit Police Scotland in this regard."

Q5. Have you conducted research into Police Scotland? What kind of work do you expect to be doing, if your application is successful?

As we've mentioned, Police Scotland want to know that their candidates have conducted thorough research before application. The last thing they want is to hire someone who will quit within 2 weeks, because they didn't know what they were getting into. Conducting research also shows a sustained interest in the role. So, use your research here to provide them with a great answer!

Sample Response

"I believe the work I would undertake will be extremely diverse and varied in nature, and that the role would require me to use a wide remit of skills and expertise. To begin with, I would be acting as a positive role model for Police Scotland, by behaving with honesty and integrity; and delivering a service to the public that exceeds their expectations.

I would be required to attend and protect crime scenes, and also investigate incidents through effective policing and by also following my training and operational procedures at all times. I would make arrests when appropriate, complete custody procedures and also interview suspects and present evidence in court.

I would liaise and work with other stakeholders and agencies, to make sure that we all worked towards the common goal of protecting the community in which we serve. I would also be required to put vulnerable people, victims of crime and witnesses first. I would be required to face challenging and difficult situations on a daily basis, and I would need to be at my best at all times to ensure I uphold the principles of policing."

Vetting Form

Following the application form, you'll need to complete a vetting form. This is essentially an in-depth form which asks you for details about areas such as your marital status, personal character and previous employment. All applicants to Police Scotland will be vetted extremely carefully, as it's important for the service to make sure that they are hiring the right type of person.

Here are the different sections of the vetting form:

Personal Details
During this section of the form you will need to fill in your personal details. You should include all of your middle names, and any

previous surnames or name changes through marriage. All information learned by the police during the vetting process will remain confidential.

You will also need to provide the police with all previous addresses during the past 10 years of your life. If you had a partner living or staying with you at said address, then you will need to tick a box acknowledging this.

Finally, you'll need to provide your work email address, any other email addresses, and your National Insurance Number.

Prior Service
In this section of the form you will need to acknowledge whether or not you have been a member of a police force before, or have served with HM forces or any other nation's military. If so, you must fill in the details of this. You must also include the details of any other government service work that you have taken part in.

Previous Application
In this section, you'll need to elaborate on whether you have ever unsuccessfully applied to join Police Scotland or another force. If so, then you will also be required to explain why you were unsuccessful with your application.

Prior Vetting
In this section you'll need to explain whether you have ever been the subject of a previous vetting procedure, by any other organisation.

Family/Domestic Circumstances
In this section of the form you'll need to fill in details about your close family. This includes details on your parents, step-parents, guardians, brothers, sister, step-siblings, children, step-children or adopted relatives, along with any other person who lives with you

– such as a flatmate, tenant or landlord.

You'll also need to list your spouse, partner or civil partner, as well as your long-term status with this partner. You'll need to tell the police when your relationship with your partner began, and also include details on any previous partners from the past 5 years of life, with from-to dates on when the relationships started and finished.

When filling in this information, you'll need to use full names for every person mentioned.

Personal Character

In this section you will need to disclose whether you have any of the following:

- A current investigation being conducted against your name, by the police or any other law enforcement body;

- Any pending court appearances, in relation to criminal charges. This includes any pending cautions or charges that would require a court appearance;

- Any past military disciplinary measures that were taken against you;

- Any disciplinary or misconduct charges resulting from previous occasions when you served in a police force;

- Any other disciplinary measures that were taken, or are in the process of being taken, against your name, by any other professional body.

Acquaintance History

In this section, you will need to disclose any criminal convictions, warnings or cautions that have been made against those who are connected to you through family or relationships. Although convictions from these people will not automatically exclude you from joining the police, they could have an impact.

Financial History

In this section, you'll need to list some details about your financial history. It's very important that candidates to Police Scotland are in a financially stable position. The reason for this is that officers who aren't in a financially stable position could be subject to exploitation by criminal groups – who are known for coercing individuals into providing them with access to confidential information. It's important to note too that just being in debt is not the issue, as Police Scotland understands that this is normal, but the key thing is that the debt is being managed in a responsible way.

First, you'll need to specify whether:

- You've ever had a credit card withdrawn, or an account defaulted;

- You've ever been the subject of a Trust Deed or Individual Voluntary Arrangement;

- You've ever been the subject of an arrestment of earnings order;

- You've ever had a loan arrangement terminated by your bank or a building society;

- You've ever been subject to repossession proceedings;

- You've ever been registered as bankrupt, or in sequestration. Applicants to whom this applies will only be considered if a period of three years has passed, since discharge of the debt. The same applies to Debt Relief Orders;

- You've ever been the subject of a Debt Management Plan, Debt Payment Programme or Debt Arrangement Scheme;

- You've ever been the subject of a negative court judgement, based on financial issues.

If any of the above apply, then you will need to provide details, figures and dates. You should study the application guidance notes, via their website, for more information on how your financial status could impact your application.

Following the above, you'll be asked to specify your current financial commitments. For example, current or joint debts, mortgages, credit agreements and credit cards. Finally, the form will ask you to give an honest answer as to whether this debt is manageable or not.

Business Ventures

In this section, you will need to list any outside business ventures that you are currently taking part in. Certain business ventures, from you and your relatives, could present an obstacle to joining the police. The form will ask you the following questions:

- Are you currently involved with any job or business interest, which you would intend to pursue following your appointment as a police officer, or a member of police staff?

The second question applies only to candidates who are applying for the role of police officer, and is as follows:

- Do you, your spouse or any relative currently living with you, own a shop or work for a business which requires a license – for example gambling, or the sale of liquor?

If the answer to any of the above questions is yes, then you will need to provide the police with full details.

Declaration

Finally, at the bottom of the form, you'll be asked to sign a declaration that all of the information you have provided is factually correct and that you've been honest. The form will also give you an extra space, in which you can enter any extra information that you think Police Scotland should know about.

Equality and Diversity Form

The next form that you will need to complete is an equality and diversity form. Police Scotland are fully committed to equality, and recognise the value of having a diverse workforce. During this form you will be asked questions surrounding your age, any disabilities, religion, etc. All answers will be kept completely confidential.

Preference Questionnaire

In this section of the form, you will be asked to indicate which Divisions you'd prefer to serve in. You'll be given a list of the available Divisions, and then will need to put a 1 next to your first choice, and a 2 next to your second choice. Police Scotland guarantees that candidates will be posted to one of their two chosen divisions, if successful.

Once all of the forms have been completed, save them out as PDF files, and then send them to the following email policeofficerrecruitment@scotland.pnn.police.uk

Now that we've covered the application form, let's move onto the SET assessment.

Standard
Entrance Test

Following the submission of your application form, provided you are successful, you'll be invited to take part in what is known as the Standard Entrance Test (SET). You'll take the SET at an assessment centre, in a location to be disclosed by Police Scotland.

The SET is a 3-paper examination, which tests you on the following areas:

* Language;

* Numbers;

* Information Handling.

In order to pass the whole SET, you will need to pass **all** three of the tests. The SET is used by all of the divisions in Scotland, so it doesn't matter which division you are applying to – you'll still have to take the test. Police Scotland is pretty generous with the SET, and candidates are given three attempts to pass. However, many candidates fall down on the numbers section in particular, so it's important to revise thoroughly beforehand.

In this chapter, we'll go through all of the above tests, and give you lots of practice on answering questions! Let's start with the language test:

SET Language

The language element of the SET will test you on areas such as grammar, spelling, punctuation, understanding of sentence structure and tenses. As we explained during the core competencies, your written communication is extremely important when working as a police officer. Therefore, it's integral for Police Scotland to test you on this before they employ you.

The language test consists of the following sections:

Section 1. Section 1 is a fairly simple grammar-based section. It is worth 12 marks in total and will contain questions based on spelling, tenses, verbs, conjunctions, prepositions, pronouns, comparatives and superlatives, and vocabulary.

Section 2. Section 2 will test your reading comprehension ability and understanding of grammar. You'll be provided with a passage, and then be required to pick 12 words out of a total of 17, to fill in gaps in the passage. Again, this section is worth 12 marks in total.

Section 3. Section 3 is pretty tricky. In this section you'll be given four jumbled-up sentences and will need to work out the correct order of the words. These sentences are deliberately difficult, and therefore it's important to stay calm and focused, and don't panic if you find them confusing initially.

Section 4. Section 4 is a direct test of your reading comprehension. You will be given 2 passages, with 6 questions following each passage. The questions will be based on what you've read. So, you need to pay close attention to all of the facts contained in the passage, and answer based on this.

Now, let's run through some practice questions, on different sections from the SET Language exam. Before each set of questions, we've given you examples to show you how to answer each of them. For the purposes of this guide, we've started out easy, and then progressed to some harder questions later on.

Practice Exercise 1: Sample Questions

Q1. Which of the following words is the odd one out?

A. Spanner

B. Pliers

C. Hammer

D. Brush

E. Drill

Answer: The answer is D – brush.

Explanation: This is because all of the other items are tools. The brush is an item used for cleaning, and therefore this is the odd one out.

Now take a look at the next sample question.

Q2. The following sentence has one word missing. Which word makes the best sense when placed in the sentence?

He had been .... for hours and was starting to lose his concentration.

A. Studying

B. Sleeping

C. Complaining

D. Walk

E. Targeting

Answer: The correct answer is **A – studying.**

Explanation: Studying is the best word here. Although some of the other words could be used in this sentence, this would be unusual. Studying is the most common term here and makes the most sense.

Using the above examples, have a go at the following questions:

Question 1

Which of the following words is the odd one out?

A. Car   B. Aeroplane   C. Truck   D. Motorbike   E. Bicycle

Question 2

Which of the following is the odd one out?

A. Flight   B. Tight   C. Alight   D. Night   E. White

Question 3

The following sentence has one word missing. Which word makes the most sense when placed in the sentence?

The mechanic worked on the car for 3 hours. At the end of the 3 hours he was _____.

A. home   B. rich   C. crying   D. exhausted   E. thinking

Question 4

The following sentence has one word missing. Which two words make the most sense when placed in the sentence?

The man _____ to walk along the beach with his dog. He threw the stick and the dog _____ it.

A.	B.	C.	D.	E.
hated/ chose	decided/ wanted	liked/ chased	hurried/ chased	hated/ loved

Question 5

In the line below, the word outside of the brackets will only go with three of the words inside the brackets to make longer words. Which one word will it NOT go with?

    A   B   C   D

In (direct famous comparable cart)

Question 6

I want to buy a new pair of jeans because I've put on _____ and my waist has expanded.

      A. wait B. weight C. wheat D. waite

Question 7

This week I felt so weak, I don't know why, maybe because I haven't _____ for days.

> A. ate   B. eat   C. hate   D. eaten

```


```

Question 8

He'll go back to his country when there is _____, but he might have to wait for years.

> A. peice   B. peece   C. peese   D. peace

```


```

Question 9

The new train was stationary for hours because of the _____.

> A. whether   B. weather   C. wether   D. weaver

```


```

Question 10

_____ country is too dangerous so they're allowed to stay here.

> A. Their   B. They're   C. There   D. Thare

```


```

Answers

1. E

2. C

3. D

4. C

5. D

6. B

7. D

8. D

9. B

10. A

Now, let's move onto some harder language questions!

Jumbled Up Sentences

Within each question you will see a jumbled up sentence. Put the brackets containing parts of the sentence in the best order for the whole sentence to make sense. Before you attempt the test, take a look at the following sample questions:

SAMPLE TEST QUESTION 1

(was sent) off Vincent (for) tackle (a) (bad).

Answer: Vincent was sent off for a bad tackle.

Note that the words in the brackets can be moved anywhere in the sentence, as long as they remain in the same order. For example, you could move 'was sent' to anywhere else in the sentence, but the words 'was sent' would need to remain in that order. You are NOT being asked to just swap the brackets around. The words that aren't in brackets cannot move. For example, in the above sentence, the word 'tackle' could never come before 'Vincent'.

As you'll see in the next example, sometimes you will have to add capital letters to the first word in the sentence, even if they are not indicated in the question:

SAMPLE TEST QUESTION 2

Valuable (my boss) the (told) in (most) the (me) I am (person) (company).

Answer: My boss told me I am the most valuable person in the company.

In the above question you should see that the words 'my boss' start the sentence, even though the 'my' inside brackets has not been capitalised. This makes things more challenging, and you'll need to spot this and rectify it within your answer.

Practice Exercise 2 Sample Questions

Within each question you will see a jumbled up sentence. Put the brackets containing parts of the sentence in the best order for the whole sentence to make sense.

Q1. I (buy) drove (some fruit) to shops to (the) vegetables (and).

Q2. (have) I (there) are many (heard that) to lemons (eating) (benefits).

Q3. I go (attending) to (that my) a party (be) but I had (wanted to) heard ex-wife would.

Q4. (woke) Scotland (the players) the (for) goal. All of (scored) celebrated, they had (final) qualified the Cup! Then I (World) up.

Q5. Eileen (wanted to) (date) Janice (in) got into a (Ted). They both (and) Ted. Unfortunately, was only (fight) interested himself.

Q6. (pens) Glenn's (illness) with him. He (up) was (chewing) diagnosed with a (habit of) terminal (finally caught).

Q7. (me that) Someone if I (superhuman) enough (drank) orange, I would (once told) develop (juice) powers.

Q8. Stanley (his house) came (his) home (watermelon) to find that (stolen) had been. The thieves (burgled) had favourite.

Q9. Gilbert (afraid) likes (his dog) at (the) night (terribly). However, (to exercise) is of dark.

Q10. I (exercise). Whenever (with an) I play (the) the (hate) wrong (book) note, my teacher (head) hits (music) me over.

Answers

1. I drove to the shops to buy some fruit and vegetables.

2. I have heard that there are many benefits to eating lemons.

3. I wanted to go to a party but I had heard that my ex-wife would be attending.

4. Scotland scored the final goal. All of the players celebrated, they had qualified for the World Cup! Then I woke up.

5. Eileen and Janice got into a fight. They both wanted to date Ted. Unfortunately, Ted was only interested in himself.

6. Glenn's habit of chewing pens finally caught up with him. He was diagnosed with a terminal illness.

7. Someone once told me that if I drank enough orange juice, I would develop superhuman powers.

8. Stanley came home to find that his house had been burgled. The thieves had stolen his favourite watermelon.

9. Gilbert likes to exercise at night. However, his dog is terribly afraid of the dark.

10. I hate music. Whenever I play the wrong note, my teacher hits me over the head with an exercise book.

Practice Exercise 3: Sample Questions

This type of question requires you to fill in the missing blank in order for the sentence to read correctly. You have a choice of 4 words with which to fill the gap in each sentence. Select the word which best completes each sentence.

Give one answer for each question. Study the examples below before you begin the exercises, to make sure you understand how to do the test.

Sample question 1

Is this the place _____ you saw the accident?

• which

• when

• where

• who

Answer: where

Sample question 2

The thief escaped _____ the open gate.

• under

• through

• over

• on

Answer: through

Now have a go at some practice questions!

Q1. The same situation kept _____ .

•   occuring

•   ocurring

•   occurring

•   ocuring

Answer [   ]

Q2. The man jumped off the ledge and broke his _____ .

- nee

- knee

- knea

- knae

Answer [   ]

Q3. Richard spent literally hours working on the same _____ of work.

- peace

- piece

- piese

- pees

Answer [   ]

Q4. Darren ate his pie too fast, and suffered from _____.

- indegestion

- indigastion

- indigestion

- indagestion

Answer

Q5. Neil looked in the mirror. He looked _____ today.

- hansome

- handsom

- handsone

- handsome

Answer

Q6. Amanda was sick of being bullied. She was going to take _____.

- acton

- actian

- action

- actien

Answer

Q7. Demi hated school. She hated the teachers, the school _____, and the students.

- dinners

- diners

- dinnerrs

- dinerrs

Answer [   ]

Q8. Martin decided that there was only one way to solve his problem. He put on a _____.

- balacalava

- balacva

- balacava

- balaclava

Answer [   ]

Q9. The student decided that he'd had enough of his teacher. He threw a _____ at her head.

- rubbor

- rubber

- rubberr

- rubbar

Answer [   ]

Q10. Patrice has decided that he doesn't want to work in publishing anymore. Instead, he's going to be an _____.

- astronot

- astronaut

- astronaught

- astronauht

Answer [   ]

Answers

1. occurring

2. knee

3. piece

4. indigestion

5. handsome

6. action

7. dinners

8. balaclava

9. rubber

10. astronaut

For hundreds more SET Language questions and exercises, check out our fantastic guide:

AVAILABLE AT WWW.HOW2BECOME.COM

SET Numbers

The next part of the SET test is a mathematical assessment. This is possibly the area where the highest number of candidates fall down. If you aren't familiar with maths or haven't practiced, then you will really struggle with this part of the test. With this in mind, you need to revise thoroughly beforehand. You will be allowed to use a calculator for this assessment, and there are 20 questions in total.

The structure of the numbers paper is as follows:

- The first 8 questions will require you to perform simple calculations, such as adding, subtracting and multiplying.

- The next 12 questions will contain a mixture of ratio questions, working out time questions, adding/subtracting money, calculating speed, distance and time, and percentages.

When taking this paper, a basic thing to remember is to always include symbols in your answers. For example, if the question asks you to add together two amounts of money, and you miss off the £ sign from your answer then you will not get the mark. This is the same for factors such as %, am/pm and weight.

Now, let's get started with some practice questions from the assessment. Just like before, we've started out with some simple questions, before moving into harder maths.

Numbers Practice Questions: Part 1

Try and answer the following 10 questions as quickly and accurately as you can. You are permitted to use a calculator for this exercise.

Q1. 18 + 26 =

Q2. 97 – 46 =

Q3. 12 x 64 =

Q4. 5 x (12 x 11) =

Q5. 74 ÷ 4 =

Q6. 4 x (4 + 5) =

Q7. 11 x (4 + 5) =

Q8. 80 ÷ 5 =

Q9. 4 x 4 x 6 =

Q10. 8 x (8 − 6) =

Answers

Q1. 44
   EXPLANATION = 18 + 26 = 44

Q2. 51
   EXPLANATION = 97 − 46 = 51

Q3. 768
   EXPLANATION = 12 x 64 = 768

Q4. 660
   EXPLANATION = 12 x 11 = 132. 5 x 132 = 660

Q5. 18.5
   EXPLANATION = 74 ÷ 4 = 18.5

Q6. 36
   EXPLANATION = 4 + 5 = 9. 4 x 9 = 36

Q7. 99

    EXPLANATION = 4 + 5 = 9. 11 x 9 = 99

Q8. 16

    EXPLANATION = 80 ÷ 5 = 16

Q9. 96

    EXPLANATION = 4 x 4 = 16. 16 x 6 = 96

Q10. 16

    EXPLANATION = 8 − 6 = 2. 2 x 8 = 16

Now that you've had a go at some easier questions, try and tackle the following tougher questions!

Numbers Practice Questions: Part 2

Q1. A wallet has been found containing one £20 note, five £5 notes, a fifty pence coin and three 2 pence coins. How much is in the wallet?

Q2. Subtract 200 from 500, add 80, subtract 30 and multiply by 2. What number do you have?

Q3. A multi-storey car park has 8 floors and can hold 72 cars on each floor. In addition to this, there are 4 allocated disable parking spaces per floor. How many spaces are there in the entire car park?

Q4. A man saves £12.50 per month. How much would he have saved after 1 year?

Q5. If there have been 60 accidents along one stretch of a motorway in the last year, how many on average have occurred each month?

Q6. Your friends tell you their electricity bill has gone up from £40 per month to £47 per month. How much extra are they now paying per year?

A. £84   B. £85   C. £83   D. £86   E. £82

Q7. A woman earns a salary of £32,000 per year. How much would she earn in 15 years?

A. £280,000 B. £380,000 C. £480,000 D. £260,000 E. £460,000

Q8. If a police officer walks the beat for 6 hours at a pace of 4km/h, how much ground will she have covered after the 6 hours is over?

A. 20km   B. 21km   C. 22km   D. 23km   E. 24km

```
┌─────────────────────┐
│                     │
│                     │
│                     │
└─────────────────────┘
```

Q9. It takes Malcolm 45 minutes to walk 6 miles to work. At what pace does he walk?

A. 7 mph   B. 4 mph   C. 6 mph   D. 5 mph   E. 8 mph

```
┌─────────────────────┐
│                     │
│                     │
│                     │
└─────────────────────┘
```

Q10. Ellie spends 3 hours on the phone talking to her friend abroad. If the call costs 12 pence per 5 minutes, how much does the call cost in total?

A. £3.30   B. £4.32   C. £3.32   D. £4.44   E. £3.44

```
┌─────────────────────┐
│                     │
│                     │
│                     │
└─────────────────────┘
```

Answers

Q1. £45.56

EXPLANATION = 20.00 + 5.00 + 5.00 + 5.00 + 5.00 + 5.00 + 0.50 + 0.02 + 0.02 + 0.02 = £45.56

Q2. 700

EXPLANATION = 500 − 200 = 300

300 + 80 − 30 = 350 x 2 = 700

Q3. 608

EXPLANATION = (8 x 72) + (4 x 8) = 576 + 32 = 608

Q4. £150

EXPLANATION = 12.50 x 12 = £150

Q5. 5

EXPLANATION = 60 ÷ 12 = 5

Q6. A = £84

EXPLANATION = In this question you need to first work out the difference in their electricity bill. Subtract £40 from £47 to be left with £7. Now you need to calculate how much extra they are paying per year. If there are 12 months in a year then you need to multiply £7 by 12 months to reach your answer of £84.

Q7. C = £480,000

EXPLANATION = The lady earns £32,000 per year. To work out how much she earns in 15 years, you must multiply £32,000 by 15 years to reach your answer of £480,000.

Q8. E = 24km

EXPLANATION = To work this answer out all you need to do is multiply the 6 hours by the 4 km/h to reach the total of 24 km. Remember that she is walking at a pace of 4 km per hour for a total of 6 hours.

Q9. E = 8mph

EXPLANATION = Malcolm walks 6 miles in 45 minutes, which means he is walking two miles every 15 minutes. Therefore, he would walk 8 miles in 60 minutes (1 hour), so he is walking at 8 mph.

Q10. B = £4.32

EXPLANATION = If the call costs 12 pence for every 5

minutes, then all you need to do is calculate how many 5 minutes there are in the 3-hour telephone call. There are 60 minutes in every hour, so therefore there are 180 minutes in 3 hours. 180 minutes divided by 5 minutes will give you 36. To get your answer, just multiply 36 by 12 pence to reach your answer of £4.32.

How did you get on with the above questions? Once you think you've fully understood them, have a go at our third and final section.

Numbers Practice Questions: Part 3

Q1. There are 400 cows in the barn. The ratio of cows to sheep, is 20:5. How many sheep are there?

Answer

Q2. Due to riots in the town of Ficshire, the western gate to the city was locked between the hours of 23:40 on Thursday, and 14:00 on Saturday. People were without food and water for a sustained period of time. How long was the western gate locked for? Give your answer in hours and minutes.

Answer

Q3. There are 2 circles, 1 triangle and a rhombus. How many individual 360 angles are there?

Answer

Q4. Martin ate dinner in his local restaurant. The restaurant charges on a time spent basis. The charge is £15.50 per hour. Martin spent 3 hours at the restaurant, before going home and arguing with his wife Maureen. How much did the restaurant charge Martin?

Answer

Q5. Daisy and Emily went on holiday to Barbados. They arrived on the 6th July, and left on the 8th August. How many days were they on holiday for?

Answer

Q6. A local running club charges £4 per adult to use the facilities, and £2 per child. On Sunday there were 18 adults who used the running club, and 3 children. How much money did the running club make on Sunday?

Answer

Q7. Miranda visits the supermarket every Monday. She needs £78.50 to cover the entire week's worth of food. On average, what is the value of food that Miranda consumes per day? Round your answer to the nearest pound.

Answer

Q8. A prison guard left the door open, and now 64% of the prisoners from Ficshire Security Centre have escaped. There are

1560 prisoners left. How many prisoners were there originally? Work out your answer to the nearest whole prisoner.

Answer [   ]

Q9. Jason became ill on Monday. He went to bed on Monday night at 8pm, and then woke up on Tuesday, 14 hours later.

Answer [   ]

Q10. Elizabeth runs a day care service. She has 15 toys at her day care centre. Today, Elizabeth is looking after five children. She wants to give them some toys to play with, whilst she takes a nap. One of the toys is broken, so this cannot be given out.

The children are named Benjamin, Sarah, Janice, Pete and Wallace.

The ratio of toys being shared amongst the children is 1:5:6:1:1

How many toys did each child get?

Answer [   ]

Answers

Q1. 80

EXPLANATION = 400 / 25 = 16. 16 x 5 = 80. Therefore, there are 80 sheep.

Q2. 38 hours and 20 minutes

EXPLANATION = Answer: 38 hours and 20 minutes.

23:40 plus 20 minutes would give you 00:00 Friday. Plus 24 hours would give you 00:00 Saturday, plus 14 hours would give you 14:00 Saturday. Add the 24, plus the 14, plus the 20 minutes, and you get the answer.

Q3. 2

EXPLANATION = The two circles are the only shapes in the list with an individual 360 degree angle.

Q4. £46.50

EXPLANATION = Martin spent 3 hours at the restaurant, with each hour costing £15.50. £15.50 x 3 = £46.50

Q5. 33 days

EXPLANATION = From the 6th July till the 8th August = 33 days.

Q6. £78

EXPLANATION = £18 x 4 = £72. £2 x 3 = £6. £72 + £6 = £78

Q7. £11

EXPLANATION = Divide Miranda's weekly spend on a per-day basis, so £78.50 divided by 7 = £11

Q8. 4450

EXPLANATION = 1602 / 36 = 44.5, which = 1%. So 44.5 x 100 = 4450.

Q9. Tuesday, 10am

EXPLANATION = Monday night 8pm + 14 hours = 10am Tuesday morning

Q10. Benjamin 1, Sarah 5, Janice 6, Pete 1, Wallace 1.

EXPLANATION = The ratio is already worked out for you, since the numbers given equal the amount of toys available.

For hundreds more SET Number questions and exercises, check out our fantastic guide:

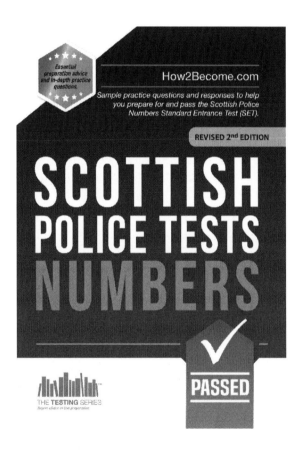

AVAILABLE AT WWW.HOW2BECOME.COM

Information Handling

The final part of the SET is the Information Handling assessment. Along with the numbers paper, this is the part of the assessment that candidates tend to find the most tricky, and many people will fall down when it comes to this. There are lots of reasons for why this test is so hard. Foremost among these, is that the style of test is something that most people won't be used to. You'll be given lots of tables and charts, and will need to answer questions based on the information within these. Fear not though. While the test is really difficult, you can practice for it, and that's where we are here to help! You will be allowed to use a calculator for this assessment.

The information handling test runs on a six-monthly rotation. This means that every 6 months, Police Scotland swap the test out for a new one. They have 3 tests in rotation at the moment, with all of the tests differing in difficulty and style. This is deliberate. Although Police Scotland want you to prepare, they also want to see how well you can deal with unexpected information.

Top Tips For Information Handling

In order to pass the Information Handling assessment, you will need to score at least 16 out of 24. There are two different types of question in this assessment, observation questions and calculation questions.

Generally, most people find that observation questions are a bit easier than calculation questions, but you still need to focus your preparation equally on the two areas.

Typical observation questions will look like this:

- On what are the most people likely to drive to the supermarket?
- Between what times were the most crimes committed?
- What is the most likely crime for people between the ages of

30-40 to commit?

Typical calculation questions will look like this:

- On average, how many armed robberies were committed per day, in the month of June?

- How many more people that stole cars were over the age of 40, than under the age of 40?

- Calculate the number of people who committed benefit fraud in the month of April, as a percentage of all the crimes committed during the year.

As we have mentioned, the style of the questions and structure regularly changes. Therefore, before applying, you should check with Police Scotland about what type of questions you can expect to face.

On the next page we've included a sample question, and following that a series of extra practice questions.

SAMPLE INFORMATION HANDLING TEST

Study the graph carefully then answer questions 1 - 6

Shoplifting by month and location

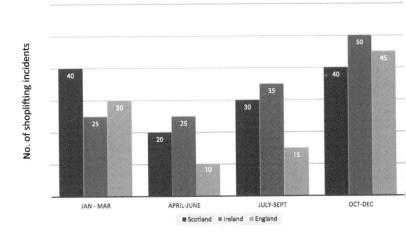

Q1. In which months did the most shoplifting occur?

Q2. In which location did the most shoplifting occur?

Q3. In total, how many shoplifting incidents happened between Jan-Mar?

Q4. In total, how many shoplifting incidents happened in England?

Q5. From January to December, how many shoplifting incidents occurred in Scotland?

```
┌─────────────────────┐
│                     │
│                     │
└─────────────────────┘
```

Q6. How many shoplifting incidents were there in total?

```
┌─────────────────────┐
│                     │
│                     │
└─────────────────────┘
```

Answers

Q1. Oct-Dec

Q2. Ireland

Q3. 95

Q4. 100

Q5. 130

Q6. 365

INFORMATION HANDLING TEST EXERCISE 1

Study the graph carefully then answer questions 1 – 6

No. of burglaries by time and day

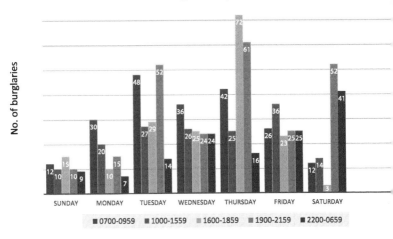

Q1. What day of the week are most burglaries committed?

Q2. On what day are burglaries least likely to be committed?

Q3. How many burglaries are committed on Friday between 10:00 – 15:59?

Q4. On what day and between what times are burglaries mostly committed?

```
┌─────────────────────┐
│                     │
│                     │
└─────────────────────┘
```

Q5. How many burglaries are committed in total between the hours of 07:00 and 09:59?

```
┌─────────────────────┐
│                     │
│                     │
└─────────────────────┘
```

Q6. How many burglaries were committed in total?

```
┌─────────────────────┐
│                     │
│                     │
└─────────────────────┘
```

INFORMATION HANDLING TEST EXERCISE 2

Study the graph carefully then answer questions 1 - 6

Children's favourite animals

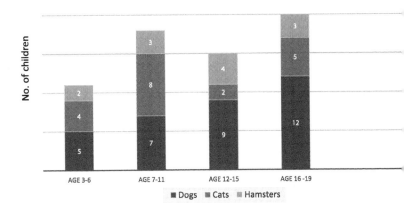

Q1. What is the most popular animal between the ages of 7 and 11?

Q2. Amongst all ages, how many children chose cats as their favourite animal?

Q3. Which age group were hamsters least popular with?

Q4. How many children took part in the survey?

```
┌─────────────────────┐
│                     │
│                     │
└─────────────────────┘
```

Q5. What is the least popular animal between the ages of 12 and 15?

```
┌─────────────────────┐
│                     │
│                     │
└─────────────────────┘
```

Q6. What animal was most popular?

```
┌─────────────────────┐
│                     │
│                     │
└─────────────────────┘
```

INFORMATION HANDLING TEST EXERCISE 3

Study the graph carefully then answer questions 1 - 6

Music preferences

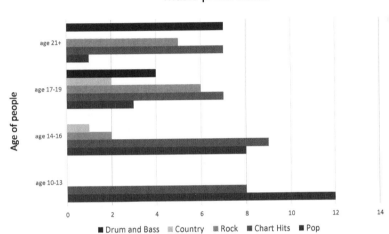

Q1. What was the most popular music choice between the ages of 14 and 16?

Q2. How many people liked country music?

Q3. In total, how many people liked drum and bass music?

Q4. What was the least popular music category?

Q5. What was the most popular music category?

Q6. Between the ages of 10 and 16, how many people liked chart hit music?

INFORMATION HANDLING TEST EXERCISE 4

Study the graph carefully then answer questions 1 - 6

No. of films released and the genre

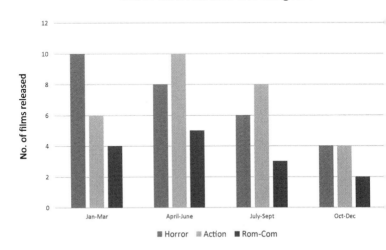

Q1. What was the most commonly released film genre between the months of July and September?

[   ]

Q2. Over the 12 month period, what genre was released the least?

[   ]

Q3. How many action films were released between January and September?

[   ]

Q4. How many rom-com films were released in total?

Q5. How many films were released between April and June?

Q6. How many films were released in the 12 month period?

INFORMATION HANDLING TEST EXERCISE 5

Study the graph carefully then answer questions 1 - 6

Types of crimes committed in a 12 month period

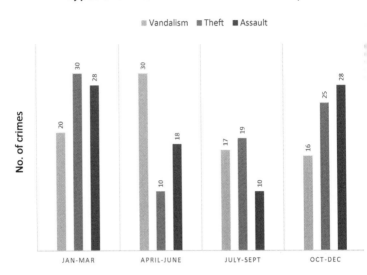

Vandalism　Theft　Assault

Q1. Between January and March, how many crimes were committed in total?

Q2. How many crimes were committed between April and June?

Q3. In total, how many crimes committed were vandalism?

Q4. How many assaults were there between January and September?

Q5. How many crimes were committed in total?

Q6. What was the least committed crime?

ANSWERS TO INFORMATION HANDLING TEST EXERCISE 1

Q1. Thursday

Q2. Sunday

Q3. 36

Q4. Thursday between the hours of 1600 and 1859

Q5. 206

Q6. 916

ANSWERS TO INFORMATION HANDLING TEST EXERCISE 2

Q1. Cats

Q2. 19

Q3. 3-6

Q4. 64

Q5. Cats

Q6. Dogs

ANSWERS TO INFORMATION HANDLING TEST EXERCISE 3

Q1. Chart hits

Q2. 3

Q3. 11

Q4. Country

Q5. Chart hits

Q6. 17

ANSWERS TO INFORMATION HANDLING TEST EXERCISE 4

Q1. Action

Q2. Rom-com

Q3. 24

Q4. 14

Q5. 23

Q6. 70

ANSWERS TO INFORMATION HANDLING TEST EXERCISE 5

Q1. 78

Q2. 58

Q3. 83

Q4. 56

Q5. 251

Q6. Vandalism

For hundreds more SET Information Handling questions and exercises, check out our fantastic guide:

AVAILABLE AT WWW.HOW2BECOME.COM

Initial Interview

If you successfully pass the SET, then you will be invited to attend an initial interview. This interview will take place with two members of your local recruitment team. During this interview, you will face competency-based questions. The competencies examined here will be as follows:

- Team work;

- Personal effectiveness;

- Effective communication;

- Respect for diversity;

- Personal awareness;

- Service delivery;

- Job knowledge.

Prior to attending this interview, it's extremely important that you conduct substantial research and preparation. Police Scotland will expect you to demonstrate that you have an understanding about the role, the service's values and purpose, and what their priorities are. Police Scotland also highly encourages candidates to visit their local station, and talk with currently serving officers about the role and what it involves.

Now, let's discuss competency-based questions, and how to go about answering them.

Competency-Based Questions

Competency-based questions are becoming more and more common in job interviews, and therefore it's essential that you are prepared for how to answer them. A competency-based question is one which focuses on a specific competency, and how you've used the competency in the past. For example, you might be asked:

Give us an example of a time when you have demonstrated good team working skills.

Here, the question takes a very direct approach, directly referencing the competency. However, not all of the questions will be this obvious. You might be asked something like:

Do you see yourself as someone who works well with others? What attributes do you have that make you a good colleague?

This question is asking roughly the same thing, but the question is a bit more subtle, and requires you to think a bit harder about what is being asked. You still need to demonstrate a past example of when you've used that behaviour, and a knowledge of how it applies to the job role.

When answering competency-based questions, it's really important that you do not fall into the trap of providing a 'generic' response that details what you 'would do' if the situation arose, unless of course you have not been in this type of situation before. Instead, you need to say what you DID do.

When responding to situational questions, try to structure your responses in a logical and concise manner. The way to achieve this is to use the 'STAR' method of interview question response construction:

Situation. Start off your response to the interview question by explaining what the 'situation' was and who was involved.

Task. Once you have detailed the situation, explain what the 'task' was, or what needed to be done.

Action. Now explain what 'action' you took, and what action others took. Also explain why you took this particular course of action.

Result. Explain to the panel what you would do differently if the same situation arose again. It is good to be reflective at the end of your responses. This demonstrates a level of maturity and it will also show the panel that you are willing to learn from every experience.

Finally, explain what the outcome or result was following your actions and those of others. Try to demonstrate in your response that the result was positive because of the action you took.

The majority of the questions will require you to focus on just one competency. As long as you fully demonstrate the competency that is being asked for in the question, then you will score good marks. You shouldn't try to force extra competencies into your answers. However, if it can be done naturally, then it's always a good idea to demonstrate these. For example, if you are answering a question about leadership, then it's completely normal for other competencies to come up too when recounting your behaviour. Likewise, while the questions will generally focus on just one competency, the interviewers will expect you to show other competencies where possible. For example, if they give you a question about leadership, then it's highly likely that competencies such as communication will need to be factored into your response.

Now, let's look at some sample questions and responses. To help you practice, we've given you a sample question and response from each of the competencies listed above. We've also explained why the competency is important, and how it's relevant to Police Scotland.

Sample Questions

Q1. Can you give me an example of when you have worked as part of a team to successfully resolve an issue?

Starting out with a very simple one, this question is obviously questioning you directly on your **team-working skills.** Think about all of the aspects that go into working as part of a team, and how you demonstrated your ability to work with others. Make sure you explain exactly what the issue was, how the group overcame it, and what your role was.

Write your answer in the textbox below, and then compare it to our response!

Sample Response

'When I was working in my previous position as an administrator, I was required to work in teams on a daily basis. Often, I was positioned as the leader of these teams. On one occasion that I can remember, our task was to organise a company-wide event. This would involve hiring out independent entertainment workers, food suppliers, health and safety specialists and other essential staff. I was one of three sub-leaders of the team and had around 30 people under my command.

My main priority was finding the relevant healthy and safety staff. I did this because health and safety at such an event should be a top priority. It is the responsibility of the company to ensure that they have met recognised safety standards, and to maintain the wellbeing of all attendees at their event. Also, in the event of an injury, a failure to implement health and safety procedures could seriously damage the business. I made contact with the paramedical department of the local hospital, and requested if they could free up several members of staff and at least two vehicles, for the day of the event. I then liaised with both of the other team leaders, to ensure that I had all of the details of exactly what they were planning. I paid particular attention to the entertainments organiser. Between us, we worked out exactly which health and safety procedures would need to be put in place to accommodate the activities being arranged.

Following this meeting, I instructed the team under my control to make contact with the local fire service, and the local police service, and request for staff members from each sector to be available on the day of the event. We successfully negotiated a time and fee. The event was a tremendous success and there were no serious injuries to report. At the end of the event, I was congratulated by my boss on my efforts in securing the participation of these crucial safety management services."

Q2. Tell me about a time when you have demonstrated your personal effectiveness.

In this question, the interviewer is asking you (directly) to demonstrate examples of when you have been effective in resolving an issue in the workplace. This is essentially what personal effectiveness comes down to – how well you can do your job. How effective are you at resolving problems?

Write your answer in the textbox below, and then compare it to our response!

Sample Response

"I am currently working as a sales assistant for a well-known retailer More recently I achieved a temporary promotion and was required to manage the shop one busy Saturday afternoon.

At approximately 2pm, a customer entered the shop and approached the desk. He began complaining to a member of staff (Julie) about a coat he had purchased from our company the week before. As Julie listened to his complaint he started to get quite irate and began to raise his voice. I could see Julie becoming upset. The gentlemen then started to be verbally abusive towards her. At that point I stepped in and calmly intervened.

First, I introduced myself as the sales assistant and informed the gentleman that I would be dealing with his complaint from here on in. I then went on to tell him that I would do all I could to resolve his complaint, but that I would not tolerate any form of aggressive, confrontational or abusive language.

I also warned him that any further use of such communication would be reported to the police, in line with company policy. This immediately had the effect of calming down the customer, as he realised that he had already crossed the line with his comments to the other member of staff. He immediately apologised to Julie.

I then asked the customer to explain exactly what had happened and reassured him that I would resolve the issue. Whilst he explained his complaint I maintained an open and relaxed body position in order to diffuse any potential conflict and utilised effective listening skills. The complaint in question was that the coat the man had purchased had ripped, after only one day of wearing it. Furthermore, it had ripped whilst he was out, leaving him to walk around for the day in the cold. This was the reason that he was so angry. After listening carefully to his complaint I then explained how I would resolve it for him. I fetched he manager and suggested that, in line with company policy, the customer should receive a replacement coat, and a full refund for his rouble. My manager agreed with me, and we returned to the man with our intended solution.

Once he had heard our solution, the customer was very pleased, and again apologised sincerely to Julie. I feel that throughout the situation, I maintained a resilient and professional stance, yet still managed to resolve the customer's complaint to their satisfaction."

Q3. Can you give an example of when you have utilised your communication skills, to deliver bad news?

This is an interesting question, and hopefully gives you some idea of how the police might use the competencies to ask a particular question, rather than just asking you whether you can demonstrate them in a straightforward manner.

Unfortunately, being a police officer means that there are times when you'll be required to break bad news to members of the public. This can be emotionally taxing, and is one of the hardest parts of the role. It will constitute a huge test of your communication skills, and you will need to be extremely sensitive and professional when placed in this position. Police officers must be capable of communicating with everyone however, and therefore it's integral that you can behave in an appropriate manner.

Write your answer in the textbox below, and then compare it to our response!

Sample Response

"Sadly, yes, this was something I had to deal with last year. The people involved were my elderly next-door neighbours. They had a cat that they had looked after for years and they were very fond of it. I had to inform them that their cat had just been run over by a car in the road. I was fully aware of how much they loved their cat and I could understand that the message I was about to tell them would have been deeply distressing. They had cherished the cat for years and to suddenly lose it would have been a great shock to them.

To begin with I knocked at their door and ask calmly if I could come in to speak to them. Before I broke the news to them I made them a cup of tea and sat them down in a quiet room away from any distractions. then carefully and sensitively told them that their cat had passed away following an accident in the road. At all times I took into account their feelings and I made sure I delivered the message sensitively and in a caring manner.

I took into account where and when I was going to deliver the message. It was important to tell them in a quiet room away from any distraction so that they could grieve in peace. I also took into account the tone in which I delivered the message and I also made sure that I was sensitive to their feelings. I also made sure that I would be available to support them after I had broken the news.

The next day, following the incident, I went round to check on the couple to see how they were feeling. Whilst they were still extremely sad, they informed me that they were grateful for the way I had treated them and that I had been so sensitive to the issue."

Q4. Tell me about a time when you noticed a member of your team behaving in an unacceptable manner.

This question is essentially asking you to confirm that you have what it takes to challenge poor behaviour. Notice that the question doesn't ask you to demonstrate that you challenged this behaviour, but of course it would reflect very poorly on you if you didn't, and therefore you need to show that you did.

The competency that you use here will very much depend on the situation, but a good example would be **respect for diversity**. You might have noticed someone behaving unacceptably towards another colleague, or even a member of the public. This question is your chance to demonstrate that you will stand up for what is right, and take action, when required.

Write your answer in the textbox below, and then compare it to our response!

Sample Response

"Whilst working as a sales person for my previous employer, I was serving a lady who was from an ethnic minority background. I was helping her to choose a gift for her son's 7th birthday when a group of our youths entered the shop and began looking around at the goods we had for sale. They began to make racist jokes and comments to the lady. I was naturally offended by the comments and was concerned for the lady to whom these comments were directed. Any form of bullying and harassment is not welcome in any situation and I was determined to stop it immediately and protect the lady from any more harm.

The lady was clearly upset by their actions and I too found them both offensive and insensitive. I decided to take immediate action and stood between the lady and the youths to try to protect her from any more verbal abuse or comments. I told them in a calm manner that their comments were not welcome and would not be tolerated. I then called over my manager for assistance and asked him to call the police before asking the four youths to leave the shop. I wanted to diffuse the situation as soon as possible, being constantly aware of the lady's feelings. I was confident that the shop's CCTV cameras would have picked up the four offending youths and that the police would be able to deal with the situation. After the youths had left the shop I sat the lady down and made her a cup of tea whilst we waited for the police to arrive. I did everything that I could to support and comfort the lady and told her that I would be prepared to act as a witness to the racial bullying and harassment that I had just witnessed.

I believe the people acted as they did because of a lack of understanding, education and awareness. Unless people are educated and understand why these comments are not acceptable, then they are not open to change. They behave in this manner because they are unaware of how dangerous their comments and actions are. They believe it is socially acceptable to act this way, when it certainly isn't.

I also feel strongly that if I had not acted and challenged the behaviour the consequences would be numerous. To begin with I would have been condoning this type of behaviour and missing an opportunity to let the offenders know that their actions are wrong (educating them) I would have also been letting the lady down, which would have in turn made her feel frightened, hurt and unsupported. We all have the opportunity to help stop discriminatory behaviour and providing we ourselves are not in any physical danger, then we should take positive action to stop it."

Q5. Can you give me an example of a time when you have improved the way you work, using the feedback of others?

This question wants you to demonstrate that you have the ability to listen to feedback and take it on board, and then use it in a constructive manner. The most relevant competency here would be **personal awareness**. Personal awareness means accepting constructive criticism from others, recognising that everyone makes mistakes, and learning from your own errors. It's very important that police officers are able to do this – because only by accepting our own flaws can we improve.

Write your answer in the textbox below, and then compare it to our response!

Sample Response

I am someone who is able to take criticism extremely well, and always do my best to handle it in as constructive a manner as possible. I believe this is something that originally resulted from my university degree, where I was subjected to large amounts of criticism and honest feedback. As a result, I have developed thick skin, and am now able to use constructive feedback to my advantage.

A good example of this was during my previous position as a History teacher. One of my lessons was observed by my head of department. This was a yearly observation, which was conducted during regular lesson time, with the aim of assessing the continuous quality of members of staff at the school.

Although I felt that the lesson went really well, my head of department had a few things to give feedback on, that she felt I could improve. I was surprised by this, but I took her feedback with an open mind and fully accepted the comments.

Her primary concern was that I was perhaps pushing the students in my class a little too hard. As she correctly pointed out, we were not due to cover the area of the curriculum that I had been teaching for another week. Feeling that my class were up to the challenge, I had rushed ahead early for this. I agreed with her that I had overestimated the group, who were not quite ready for the new material. I have a tendency to be a little too enthusiastic with pushing the learning boundaries of my pupils.

While this can pay off, and there are good intentions behind it, I accept that there is a time and a place for this. Using the feedback provided, I made immediate changes to my next lesson, which had involved trying to incorporate the same approach. I was flexible enough to recognise that I had made a mistake and learned from the feedback from my head of department.

Although I am a highly-experienced professional, I am still capable of improvement and absolutely welcome the opportunity to do so."

Q6. Can you give me an example of a time when you have provided a great level of service to a customer?

One of the foremost priorities for any police officer should be in delivering a great level of service to the customer – which in this case would be the general public. So, with this in mind, it's imperative for Police Scotland that you can demonstrate your ability to do this. Remember that as an employee of Police Scotland, you are a representative of the service. The police are expected to behave in an exemplary fashion, and this means doing your utmost to ensure that the general public feel safe and protected.

Write your answer in the textbox below, and then compare it to our response!

Sample Response

"I currently work for a utility services company. We provide safe installation of key workplace and home utilities – such as boilers, radiators and plumbing.

Most recently I was asked to install new gas boilers in four properties within a tight deadline. The work would be done on a building site, close to our HQ. Whilst I understood it was important to carry out the task quickly, there was no way I was going to compromise on safety. I started off by creating a mini action-plan in my head which detailed how I would achieve the task. I set about installing the first boiler conscientiously and carefully whilst referring to the safety manual when required. I made sure that there was sufficient ventilation in the houses as required under health and safety law.

During the week that I was required to complete the task I had previously arranged to go to a birthday party with my wife, but I decided to cancel our attendance at the event as I needed to get a good night's sleep after each hard day's work. I knew that if I was to maintain the concentration levels required to work safely and achieve the task then I would need to be in tip-top condition and getting sufficient rest in the evenings was an important part of this. By the end of the fourth day I had successfully completed the task that was set by the foreman and the proceeding safety checks carried out by the inspector on the boilers proved that I had done a very good job."

Police Scotland: Assessment Centre

If you successfully pass the initial interview, then you will be invited to attend an assessment centre. The assessment centre will be held at an undisclosed location, and you'll be joined by everyone else who passed the interview too. If you aren't familiar with attending assessment centres, they are essentially a day of testing and challenges, designed to highlight the very best candidates. During your Police Scotland assessment day, you will take the following exercises:

- 3 practical, group exercises;

- 1 competency-based interview.

In this chapter, we'll give you an overview of what each of the above entails, and some fantastic tips on how to pass them!

Group Exercises

During the assessment centre you will be asked to take 3 practical exercises. All of the exercises will be group-based tasks, which place an emphasis on teamwork and co-ordination, as well as your understanding of the core competencies. During the group exercises, you will be expected to demonstrate the following competencies:

- Effective communication;

- Personal effectiveness;

- Team working;

- Respect for diversity;

- Personal awareness;

- Problem solving.

Group activities may also range from the cerebral (using the group o think) to the physical (and this could be anything from the less strenuous building a tower from spaghetti, to the more testing issue of swinging from ropes). Group activities are usually included in an assessment centre to test how you perform within a group situation – how you decided on your place within the group and how you interact with others. Today it is accepted that mechanical skills and knowledge are not enough by themselves; they are only part of the story. Very few people work in isolation and the ability to work with others, motivate and tap into their idea streams are key. This is especially important in the police, where your ability to work with others could have a direct impact on issues such as crime rate, and the welfare of members of the public.

Group activities consider more than just communication, they reveal:

The dynamics that go on between people and how you react;

How you deal with conflict;

Whether you can instigate ideas;

How obstructive you might be;

How you respond to the ideas of others;

Whether you are a leader or follower;

The extent to which you are able to build on other ideas;

The amount to which you are compliant and willing to go with the group.

In essence, group activities are designed to test how you react in people-focused situations, and put you under some form of pressure. We can all be on our best behaviour while the world is ordered and things are going well, but very often we revert to type under pressure. It is when we are under pressure that we see how short a person's temper really is, or how they handle discord in the group. As you'll know from reading this book, it's very important that police officers can maintain a calm and composed outlook and stay in control of their emotions.

What do group activities involve?
Naturally, there are an enormous number of group exercises that you could potentially encounter. This means that while we can't give you the specific details of exactly what exercises Police Scotland will ask you to take, we can provide you with lots of examples of commonly used group exercises, all of which will utilise the same skillset.

Here's the usual format of a group exercise:

First of all you will be given a scenario and you may also be given roles. You are expected to conduct a meeting or take part in the activity in the role of that person and represent whatever company your role play asks of you. If you are given a role, then be assured that everyone else will be too. You may also be given additional papers to read through.

You will then be asked to enter a room, which is usually laid out with a largish area in the middle where you will enact the activity (there may be a table and chairs) and several chairs with their backs against the walls. The chairs against the wall, facing inwards, are for your observers, and they may even be sitting there when you enter the room. These observers are the assessors for this activity. They will be watching you intently throughout the activity and will mark significant facts regarding your comments, body language and behaviour on sheets of paper throughout the activity.

The observers will not speak to you throughout the entire activity and often remain in the room even after you have left. You may find that they do not even make eye contact with you; they endeavour to stay as neutral as possible. Take a seat around the table (if there is one). It is also helpful to pretend that you do not know the other people present, so that you start with introductions. This enables you instantly to get to know who the other 'players' are in this part of the assessment centre, and who (and what) they are representing. From this you will begin to draw conclusions, for example it is likely that the finance manager has some money and that others around the table will be competing for it – but keep an open mind, these are only tentative ideas at this stage.

Enact the activity as you would in real life. You will find that as you progress you will be drawn into the activity and this is where your real behaviour is shown, but it is best to try to remember that you are being assessed at all times.

From time to time you will see the observers writing things down. This can feel very similar to a driving test where it is automatically intimidating to see someone so near, noting something down – but please try to relax. They may simply be writing comments such as 'good eye contact' and so it is best to try to ignore all scribblings as much as possible.

After a set period of time, perhaps an hour, the activity will be stopped whether you have made the decision, solved the problem or finished the meeting. The objective from the observer's point of view is to see you in action and they will have seen plenty of you in an hour! At this point you will probably be asked to leave the room to have a break, while the assessors retire to write up their notes and confer.

But very briefly then, the process is:

1. You may be given information or a role (if so read thoroughly)

2. You will be asked to enter the room and sit down.

3. You will be observed undertaking a group activity and marked on your language, body language, content and style.

4. You will be stopped after a set amount of time.

5. You will leave the room.

Now, let's have a look at some group exercises that you might encounter. While we can't give you the exact details of what exercises you will sit at the assessment centre – since there are an enormous range of group activities that you might be asked to take, we can provide you with some sample exercises, which test the same skills.

Team Meetings

These aim to replicate a typical team meeting. If this is chosen then you will be given an agenda and some notes. You will also need to know what type of team it is and whether there are any issues that need addressing within the meeting.

The assessors will be looking for a team or collaborative approach and therefore you will not receive favour for flaring up or setting yourself (or other team members) against one another or the rest of the team. Also, if you have been given an issue to address (such as excessive sickness), make sure you do this, and don't skirt around the issue or run out of time.

If you are truly going to manage a team and deliver on your targets through and with these people, they need to look up to you and see leadership at the most and mutual respect at the least. This MUST be exhibited through every part of your communication and hat means your actions (even when you think no one is looking). Therefore totally rule out any rolling of the eyes, sarcastic looks, aughing at others contributions, or staring out of the window.

Problem Solving Groups

This form of group activity will present you with a problem that you are expected to solve. The big mistake that most people make here is that they concentrate on solving the problem – well that s hardly surprising as that is what you are here for isn't it? Well no actually. If you solve the problem in the allotted time, well and good, but actually you are being assessed on your behavioural skills too. In fact quite often the problem is one that cannot easily be solved and therefore the most you can do is make headway with the group.

Although it is important to work on the problem, what you are being judged on is just HOW you do that. A good aide memoire for any problem solving situation is to remember the problem solving triangle shown below:

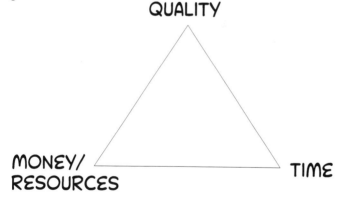

These factors can be independently manipulated to solve most problems. For example if you are working in a publishing company and are looking of new ways to reduce the cost of publishing a new catalogue of your books, you could look at:

- Adjusting the quality – use cheaper paper, include less pictures of covers, reduce the number of pages, or even produce it on line.

- Money/resources – could you divert some more money from another project to this to retain the quality, after all this is an income generating project and the shop-front for you business? Do we need to assess how potential loss of sales could correlate to the brochure (for example if every £10 on brochure price nets £50 of sales wouldn't it be worth paying?

- Time – time costs money. Would we save money (that could then be invested) if we were able to reduce the amount of time spent on this project? Would it be cheaper if we actually took longer over the project (you often pay for speed such as in cases of delivery)? How about if the brochures were produced abroad and transported via the cheapest route?

As you can see all areas could be adjusted either up or down and having this picture in your mind will enable you to have something to work to in the meeting and free you up from worrying about something to say, therefore enabling you to concentrate instead on how you interact with everyone.

OK, so you now have that model in your back pocket – how should you approach this exercise?

After the general introductions, see if anyone would like to chair the meeting and suggest an appropriate process or structure for the task. If no one comes forward then suggest yourself.

You need to start off by looking at the problem. Why is it a problem? For whom? What impact does this have on the business? Find out how it impacts on each person and their business area by asking everyone to comment on where they see issues with the problem from their own business perspective.

Explore where there are unknowns and assumptions (because this is likely to be a role play exercise) and put those up on flip chart if possible. Get everyone to contribute towards possible solutions and if you are the chair, steer the discussion. However, if you are not the chair you will need to demonstrate your realms of influence by suggesting a structure or way forward for the meeting.

Therefore:

1. The race is not on to find the quickest solution.

2. You must involve everyone in the discussions.

3. Work out first how you are going to work together as a group.

4. Make a joint plan as to how you use your time in the group (AND the process you will go through).

5. Ensure everyone has a fair chance to speak.

6. Note up on a flip chart (if there is one) everyone's ideas (and explore whether there are areas where you lack information or knowledge).

7. Don't worry if you do not get as far as solving the problem by the end of the meeting.

Decision Making Groups

Decision making is a natural partner that sits alongside problem solving, but is slightly different. Here the assessors will definitely be looking for a structured approach. It is not sufficient to make an ad hoc decision unless you are placed in a very senior position within the group.

After the general introductions see if anyone would like to chair the meeting and suggest an appropriate process or structure for the task. If no one comes forward then suggest yourself.

Decision making is not simply about coming forward with ideas, it is how you work with the ideas of others and deal with rafts of information. After all, if twelve people sit around the table and just shout out ideas, how is anyone going to manage that information? Voting for the best option is not generally a good idea, as we would all vote for our own decision. With this in mind, there has to be a structure that is agreed with the group as to how you will manage the task, including how you will make the final decision. You may well decide that everyone shouts out ideas, but if so there must be a way of weighting or measuring that information against certain criteria. This is where you will need a decision grid with the best ideas down the side and the criteria across the top. Using this method, you will be able to rate your ideas against the criteria. This gives you a logical and justifiable way of making your decision. For example, if you wanted to know which restaurant to book your Christmas luncheon at, try this:

	The Old House	The Roe Buck	Maggie's Kitchen	The Karu House
Must serve vegetarian food	✓	✓	✓	✓
Have a traditional Christmas dinner	✓	✓	✓	✗
Plenty of parking	✗	✓	✗	✓
Must be open from 12:30 until 4:00pm	✓	✓	✗	✓

You can see from the example above that the only place that you can hold the Christmas luncheon this year (according to the criteria) would be The Roe Buck because it the only choice that satisfies all the criteria. Grids such as this are used regularly for decision making as they are justifiable and aid the funnelling down and sifting of ideas that is required to come to one final decision. If there are several outcomes that meet the criteria, then you would need to suggest further study. For example if three of the four eating houses above met the criteria, then we need more criteria to enable the final decision. That might mean that another piece of work needs to take place outside of the meeting, and you would be looking for a volunteer from the group to take this forward.

Therefore:

1. The process is to broaden the subject out to collect ideas, and then later narrow it down again towards a decision.

2. You must involve everyone and try to make sure everyone contributes.

3. Process is vital, and make sure everyone agrees at every juncture.

4. Create criteria that everyone is happy with.

5. Measure the group's ideas against the criteria.

6. Look at your results and suggest a way forward.

7. Don't worry if you do not get as far as making the end decision by the end of the meeting – it is fine to suggest further work is needed.

Debating

Holding a debating group activity adds a little extra to the mix. Not only are you demonstrating how you work with others and in a group but you are also demonstrating your values and thought processes. It is almost impossible to debate a subject without giving a lot of yourself away. This can be a good thing or not depending on your views. For example, if you were to go to an assessment centre at a Pharmaceutical company you may be faced with debating 'Should animals be used for pharmaceutical testing?' Consider for one moment how you stand on this (highly emotive) subject. It would be impossible to debate this subject without revealing your core values and principles, and the debating itself may get you rather hot under the collar, whichever side of the debate you are on.

Consider also if you were asked to uphold the debate for the other side of the argument. What would you say? Would you be able to deliver? Perhaps you would find that one step too far? Only you can decide but you will be judged on your response.

Debates are often thought in terms of polar opposites but there is usually some common ground that both sides can agree on, and this should be explored and noted. We all have differing views about life's issues and you need not to appear as if an open discussion quickly becomes open combat! Neither is it OK to just have one dogged view, in a debating exercise you must be able to substantiate that view.

Therefore:

Think about your values – how do you really feel about this subject?

- If you are asked to hold a view that is not your own, consider first how this makes you feel. If you can live with it, then go with it.

- Just because it is a debate does not mean that it is an argument. It needs a structure.

- Start by asking everyone to share their views.

- Decide as a group how you are going to include everyone's ideas.

- Work together to elicit areas of common agreement.

- Remember you are still being observed – the debate is only the vehicle for a discussion. It is still a team activity.

Negotiating

Negotiating is a high-level skill and it takes any form of debating one step higher. A debate may centre on you holding your view but in a negotiation the emphasis is on persuading and influencing the other person to accept your view. For this to happen, finding that common ground on which you can agree can become even more important, for if we can find an area of agreement we can explore our difference from that point.

All managers need to negotiate and in essence all of us need to be able to undertake this skill in varying areas of our lives. For example, have you ever wanted to negotiate on the price of a car? A new house? Some furniture? Your future salary? All of these are real life situations where we need to negotiate. Doing so in a group activity is simply taking that one step further. A word to the wise: if you are thinking of annihilating your opponent here, you need to think again. You may walk away the winner but that approach is not good for long term business. The other party will feel small and insignificant and will not want to do business with you again. This approach is often called 'I win: you lose' and it is not a good outcome in business.

Let's look at the other possible outcomes:

'I lose: you win' – This is great for you as you may now feel on top of the world, feeling that you have won over me, but it is not long until I start feeling resentful. Whether I blame you for winning or myself for being weak and ill prepared, I do not feel like I want to meet with you again. I may even feel that the power ratio between us has shifted in your favour. All in all, once again not a helpful way to continue in business and a situation I would rather forget than be reminded of – and therefore I would not be seeking you out in the future (and I am sure your observer will not think well of you losing to a competitor outright – it does not bode well for the business).

lose: you lose' – In this position we both lost. Perhaps neither of us negotiated a good deal, or we failed to reach a settlement - leaving us both feeling frustrated and dissatisfied. On a positive note, if we recognise the situation in time we could adjourn or re-think our approach – possibly setting another date in the near future to come together again but any assessor observing you here would score you a very low mark.

win: you win' – This is what you should be aiming for, both parties gaining from the negotiation. The outcome may not necessarily benefit both equitably but there are positive outcomes for each. The great thing about getting to Win: Win is that it preserves the relationship. You will have no problems negotiating with this person again and that builds a solid foundation to your future working relationship – and this is why you should be aiming for this outcome.

When there are more people in the room, this becomes a lot trickier. Again you (or someone in the group) must find out what people want to get out of the negotiation. There must be some 'non-negotiables' as well as some 'concessions' – tease out these to find out where commonalities can be accommodated easily. Also try to ascertain links. For example, if there is only a small pot of money and you all want to undertake training programmes, do any of the projects link in any way? Can you share the money by sharing the training? Finally think about creative solutions. What could you get for free? The room? The trainer? Lunch? Can any of be provided in a different format? Webinars? E-learning? All of these would bring down the cost of the training programme.

At all times, remember:

> You are still in a group activity. Whatever the solution, it has to be agreed by THE GROUP.

2. Ensure everyone outlines their situation so that all the information is in the room.

3. At this point you could rate them as 'non-negotiable' and 'negotiable' if you want to write up notes.

4. Try to find those links (a clue here is that they are usually more evident in role play than in real life).

5. Work with the group to find a number of creative solutions so that everyone is helping each other with their topic/issue.

6. Re-cap the outcomes and also remember to keep involving everyone in the group to ensure they are happy with the progress.

7. For win: win to be an outcome, every member of the group should walk away with something even if it is not exactly what they wanted at the beginning.

Now that we've gone through the group exercises, let's move onto the assessment centre interview!

Assessment Centre Interview

The assessment centre interview will once again be competency based. Similarly to the initial interview, you will need to answer series of questions, but these questions will be focused around the following competencies:

• Effective communication;

• Personal effectiveness;

• Job knowledge;

• Personal awareness;

Leadership;

Partnership working.

You are likely to be asked at least one question based on each of the competencies, and it also would not be unusual for the interviewers to ask one or two motivational style questions on top of this. Just like before, when you answer these questions, you will need to use the STAR method in order to do so.

Below we have provided you with 5 sample question and responses, from the above core competencies! Place your response in the textbox below the question, and then compare it with our sample response.

Q1. Tell us about a time when you have used your communication skills to resolve a difficult problem.

Sample Response

In my previous role, I worked as a team leader at a catering company. The company had a great reputation, and are well-known nationally. Our company would be paid to organise the catering for parties and events, with different events being given to different teams within the organisation. As one of the team leaders, my role was to oversee the management of any projects that my team was given. This included making sure that the budget was kept to, motivating staff to perform at their best, and giving my team instructions on how we should allocate our resources. In order to help me manage the team, I had assigned a sub-team leader, named Michelle. Michelle would essentially act as my deputy, and would be given responsibility for taking key decisions.

On the day in question, we were preparing for an event in Wolverhampton. The event in question was a big birthday party. I sent my team to the venue to help start setting up, whilst I met with the person who was running the event, just to cross-check on key elements such as time, and food allergy requirements. When I arrived at the venue, I found that two members of the team were engaged in a furious debate. One of them was Michelle. Voices were being raised and things were getting extremely heated. This was attracting the attention of the venue staff, who looked extremely unimpressed by the situation.

I quickly stepped across, and asked Michelle and the other team member to calm down and come with me outside, so that we could resolve this. I then calmly and professionally asked them to explain what the issue was. Michelle explained to me that the team member in question was refusing to obey her instructions. She had asked him to lay out a series of fish pasties across the table on the right-hand side, but he had refused. Upon hearing this, the team member furiously interrupted. He said that we shouldn't be serving fish pasties, because some attendees would be allergic to fish. He referred to Michelle in extremely demeaning terms. Having spoken with the event manager, was fully aware of all allergy requirements – and none of the attendees were allergic to fish.

After listening to the complaints, I first addressed the team member. explained to him that the way he had spoken to Michelle was completely unacceptable, and that even if she had made a mistake, then this would not be okay. I then explained to him that he was in fact wrong, and there were no attendees who were allergic to fish. To back this up, I showed him the event listing, which contained the details of all known allergies

Once the team member saw this, he acknowledged that he had made a mistake, and apologised profusely to Michelle. He begged me not to fire him. Michelle immediately accepted his apology, and informed him that mistakes happen, and that the important thing is to move forward and resolve this. I was happy with this, and authorised the team member to get back to work."

22. Tell us about a time when you have used your job knowledge to resolve a problem.

Sample Response

"Whilst working in my previous role, as a sales assistant in a compute
shop, I was required to use my technical expertise on a number of
occasions.

One such incident occurred on a regular weekday. A customer had
come into the store, to complain that the laptop he'd brought from us
two months earlier, had crashed. The customer did not have warranty
on this laptop.

My colleague was assigned to deal with the customer. This colleague
was very new to the store, and this was his first week on the job. Upon
examining the laptop, he determined that the crash was the fault of the
individual, and was nothing to do with the store. He also said that since
the laptop was outside the returns period, there was nothing the store
could do to help him. This enraged the customer, who immediately
declared that he would be taking legal action against the store. My
colleague became upset at this, and shouted back at the customer
telling him that he looked forward to seeing him in court.

I immediately stepped in to defuse this situation. I approached my
colleague, and the customer, and asked to have a look at the laptop.
Upon further examination, I managed to locate the source of the error
and determined that this was actually a hardware issue – and therefore
was the fault of the store. Written in our sales terms and conditions
we had an agreement that we would resolve/refund hardware issues.
I informed the customer of this, and apologised wholeheartedly on
behalf of the store. I offered him a full refund, or a replacement laptop
and he seemed happy with this.

Once the customer had left the store, I took my colleague to one side
and explained why I had taken this action. I encouraged him to closely
read over the store terms and conditions, so that mistakes like this

wouldn't happen again. I also reassured him that I was confident in his ability to do the job, and would always be here to help if he needed advice."

23. Tell us about a time when you have demonstrated your leadership skills.

Sample Response

"During my previous role as an administration manager at my previous company, I was given leadership of a team of other admin workers. Our responsibilities included dealing with absences from the company, managing the finance elements of the business, and making appointments for the management team.

As the leader of the team, one of my jobs was to make sure that new staff to the department felt welcomed and integrated. On the week in question, we had two new staff members. One of them, named Eileen, was ultra-confident. She seemed very happy to take on any new tasks and was happy to work independently. The other new staff member, named Maisie, was less confident. She seemed extremely nervous, and I got the impression that she would need quite a lot of help to feel included in the company.

Although I very much wanted to keep an eye on both of them, I decided that I wanted to prioritise Maisie. Therefore, I asked another staff member if they would be happy to oversee Eileen's initial training – just to make sure that she was getting on okay. I then sat down with Maisie myself, to talk with her about integrating into the company. I calmly and professionally discussed her feelings about joining the company, about the work that she'd be doing, and the parts that she felt least confident about. Upon establishing which parts she was the least confident in, I put together an action plan. This included training on certain areas, and I also offered to run through certain elements of the job with her as she was doing them, to get her confident in the role.

We worked together for a period of three days, after which time Maisie felt confident enough to work on her own. I am pleased to say that she did really well after this, and was an exemplary member of our team.

I believe that my skills in identifying which of the new staff members needed the most help, and in which way this should be given, were crucial in ensuring that Maisie integrated fully into our team."

Q4. Can you give me an example of a time when you have worked with individuals from other organisations or groups? How did this go?

Sample Response

"Whilst working for my previous company as a member of the events team, I was part of the group responsible for managing and organising company conferences. In order to do this, we would have to make contact with the owners of the venue, as well as our client, and negotiate factors such as cost, availability and catering.

The event in question was to be a large-scale conference. Our client was an international refurbishment company, who were running the conference in order to enhance their business network. There were going to be over 500 people attending this conference, from all around the world, so it was essential that we got it right!

The first thing I did was to contact the manager of our client company. I asked him to provide me with a list of every single attendee, where they were travelling from, and whether they would have any special requirements. After the manager sent this through, I split the list into separate parts – with 100 people being sent to 5 different teams within our department. I felt that this was the best approach to managing such a huge number of people. At all times, we liased with the other teams, to make sure everyone was on the right track.

Next, I contacted another department in our company, who were in charge of dealing with issues such as reviews and feedback. I asked them to provide me with the feedback we'd had on our past events, so that I could make sure we did the same things right, and improve on any weak areas. Once they provided me with this list, I made it a priority to improve on the areas which had received negative feedback.

Following the event, which was a huge success, I arranged a meeting with the manager of our client company, to get their thoughts on how the event was run. I wanted to make sure that we worked with this client, in a collaborative fashion, to run future events. The client

eemed very happy with how the event was run, and provided us with
ustained feedback – which we took into account for the future."

**Q5. Tell me about a time when you have demonstrated a
strong level of personal awareness.**

Sample Response

"I currently work as a telecommunications engineer and I have been doing this job for nine years now. I am very well qualified, and can carry out the tasks that form part of my job description both professionally and competently. However, with the introduction of wireless telecommunications I started to feel a little bit out of my depth. Wireless telecommunications provide telephone, Internet, data, and other services to customers through the transmission of signals over networks of radio towers. The signals are transmitted through an antenna directly to customers, who use devices such as mobile phones and mobile computers to receive, interpret, and send information. I knew very little about this section of the industry and decided to ask my line manager for an appraisal. During the appraisal I raised my concerns about my lack of knowledge in this area and she agreed to my request for continuing professional training in this important area.

As part of my role, I often have to communicate directly with customers dealing with their issues and queries. Given that I was learning a variety of new things, I felt that it was my responsibility to make sure that I was fully equipped to help all of our customers out to the best of my ability.

Along with the new training that I would be provided with, I also sought out advice from my line manager on the best way to link my new skill with great customer service. Together, we ran through a plan of action that would allow me to do so.

I was soon booked on a training course which was modular in nature and took seven weeks to complete. During the training I personally ensured that I studied hard, followed the curriculum and checked with the course tutor periodically to assess my performance and act on any feedback they offered.

At the end of the training I received a distinction for my efforts. I now

elt more comfortable in my role at work and I also started to apply
or different positions within the company that involved wireless
echnology. For the last six months I have been working in the wireless
elecommunications research department for my company and have
xcelled in this new area of expertise."

Fitness
Assessment

If you successfully pass the assessment centre, then you will be invited to take part in an initial fitness test. There will be two fitness tests in total. One fitness test will take place after the assessment centre, and the other will take place prior to appointment – to ensure that you can meet the continuous fitness levels required for Police Scotland. If you fail the initial fitness assessment then you will have to wait for 6 months before you can re-apply for the role, so it's important to ace this test the first time round! Following your fitness test, the final stage is a medical, and then it's on to training.

In this chapter, we'll give you some top tips on how to prepare for the fitness test, and what you'll face during the assessment.

The Bleep Test

The Bleep Test, otherwise known as the Multi-Stage Fitness Test or the shuttle-run test, is a challenging fitness assessment. When taking part in this exercise, you will need to run continuously between two lines, set 20 metres apart, whilst a series of bleep noises plays in the background. The bleeps tell you when you can run from one line to the other. So, you need to aim to be at the next line before the next bleep sounds.

As the test goes on, the speed of the bleeps increases. If you can't reach the line before the next bleep sounds, then you'll be given a warning. If you fail to reach the line on two consecutive occasions after a warning, then the test will be over for you.

Scoring

Your performance in the bleep test will be scored based on how long you continue the test. Candidates are scored via a levelling system, which is related to how fast the bleeps are at the point where they drop out. In order to pass the Police Scotland fitness assessment, you will need to reach a score of 5.4 (in both the initial fitness test and the pre-appointment fitness test).

Below we've included some tips, on how to improve your fitness and get in shape for the bleep test.

Running Programme

One of the best ways to prepare for the fitness tests is to embark on a structured running programme.

You do not need to run at a fast pace or even run for long distances, in order to gain massively from this type of exercise. Before we provide you with the running programme however, take a read of the following important running tips.

Tips for running

As with any exercise you should consult a doctor before taking part to make sure that you are medically fit.

It is certainly worth investing in a pair of comfortable running shoes that serve the purpose for your intended training programme. Your local sports shop will be able to advise you on the types that are best for you. You don't have to spend a fortune to buy a good pair of running shoes.

It is a good idea to invest in a 'high visibility' jacket or coat so that you can be seen by fast moving traffic if you intend to run on or near the road.

Make sure you carry out at least 5 whole minutes of stretching exercises not only before but also after your running programme. This can help to prevent injury.

Whilst you shouldn't run on a full stomach, it is also not good to run on an empty one either. A great food to eat approximately 30 minutes before a run is a banana. This is great for giving you energy.

- Drink plenty of water throughout the day. Try to drink at least 1.5 litres each day in total. This will keep you hydrated and help to prevent muscle cramp.

- Don't overdo it. If you feel any pain or discomfort then stop and seek medical advice.

RUNNING PROGRAMME WEEK 1 DAY 1

- Run a total of 3 miles only at a steady pace. If you cannot manage 3 miles then try the following:

- Walk at a brisk pace for half a mile or approximately 10 minutes.

- Run for 1 mile or 8 minutes.

- Walk for another half a mile or approximately 10 minutes.

- Run for 1.5 miles or 12 minutes.

Walking at a brisk pace is probably the most effective way to lose weight if you need to. It is possible to burn the same amount of calories if you walk the same distance as if you were running. When walking at a 'brisk' pace it is recommended that you walk as fast as is comfortably possible without breaking into a run or slow jog.

RUNNING PROGRAMME WEEK 1 DAY 2

- Walk for 2 miles or approximately 20 minutes at a brisk pace

- Run for 2 miles or 14 minutes.

- Repeat DAY ONE.

- Walk at a brisk pace for 0.5 miles or approximately 7 minutes

Run for 3 miles or 20 minutes.

DAY 5

Repeat day one.

DAY 6 AND DAY 7

Rest days. No exercise.

RUNNING PROGRAMME WEEK 2 DAY 1

Run for 4 miles or 25 minutes.

DAY 2

Run a total of 3 miles at a steady pace.

you cannot manage 3 miles then try the following:

Walk at a brisk pace for half a mile or approximately 10 minutes.

Run for 1 mile or 8 minutes.

Walk for another half a mile or approximately 10 minutes.

Run for 1.5 miles or 12 minutes.

RUNNING PROGRAMME WEEK 2 DAY 3

Rest day. No exercise.

DAY 4

Run for 5 miles or 35–40 minutes.

DAY 5

Run for 3 miles or 20 minutes.

- Walk at a brisk pace for 2 miles or approximately 20 minutes

DAY 6

- Run for 5 miles or 35–45 minutes.

DAY 7

- Rest day. No exercise.

Once you have completed the second week running programme use the 3rd week to perform different types of exercises, such a cycling and swimming. During week 4 you can then commence the 2-week running programme again. You'll be amazed at how much easier it is the second time around!

When preparing for the selection process, use your exercise time as a break from your studies. For example, if you have been working on the application form for a couple of hours why not take a break and go running? When you return from your run you can then concentrate on your studies feeling refreshed.

Now that we've provided you with a structured running programme to follow, there really are no excuses. So, get out there, start running and start preparing for your multi-stage fitness assessment!

WANT MORE HELP PASSING THE SCOTTISH POLICE SELECTION PROCESS?

CHECK OUT OUR OTHER TITLES:

FOR MORE INFORMATION ON OUR TESTING SERIES, PLEASE CHECK OUT THE FOLLOWING:

WWW.HOW2BECOME.COM

Printed in Great
Britain
by Amazon